TEXAS BOUNDARIES

NUMBER FIFTY-NINE:
The Centennial Series of the
Association of Former Students,
Texas A&M University

TEXAS BOUNDARIES

Evolution of the State's Counties

Luke Gournay

Texas A&M University Press
College Station

Library of Congress Cataloging-in-Publication Data

Gournay, Luke, 1926—
    Texas boundaries : evolution of the state's counties / Luke Gournay. — 1st ed.
        p. cm. — (The centennial series of the Association of Former Students, Texas
    A&M University ; no. 59)
    Includes bibliographical references and index.
    ISBN 0-89096-653-2 (cloth); ISBN 1-58544-203-8 (pbk.)
    1. Texas—Boundaries.   2. Texas—Administrative and political divisions.
    I. Title.   II. Series.
    F392.B7G64   1995
    911'.764 — dc20   95-13850
                                                                        CIP

Contents

Maps

Preface

From twenty-three poorly defined territories called municipalities that existed in 1836, the state of Texas evolved to its present form of two hundred fifty-four organized governmental bodies that we know as Counties. This evolution can be traced in the changes in county boundaries over time. The steady progression of county maps reflects the migration of thousands of people from the United States and from numerous other countries around the world.

As the population increased and people moved westward, it became important for county courthouses and offices to be located closer to the inhabitants. In response to this need, new Counties were created from larger ones and from land districts. Every time a new county was formed, Texas had a new map. The greater part of this book tracks the reconstruction of the Texas map following the creation of such Counties.

A set of maps documenting changes in county boundaries in itself constitutes an account of the history of the region depicted. Behind the maps lie stories: about the founders of new Counties, about actions of the governmental bodies that created the Counties, about the choice of a name for each county, and about the meanings of such names. The selection of a county seat was not always a serene process, since the winning site would have a significant advantage over other candidates, in terms not only of convenience, but also of financial prosperity. Selection sometimes entailed armed conflict, with opponents frequently claiming fraud in an election.

This book explores these events and displays them in the form of maps, creating an atlas of Texas' geographical and political evolution. Each new map not only illustrates the geography of Texas at the time, but also conveys something of its passions and philosophy.

A prominent physicist, when presented with a bold new theory, once asked, "Draw a map for me so I can understand it." The same thinking applies to a surveyor's arcane—though accurate—analytical description of a piece of land: "That's fine, but show me a map so I can understand it." Maps allow us to visualize a city, a nation, or a universe more intimately, in greater detail. They have the capacity to stir our imaginations in a unique way.

Numerous people contributed ideas, time, and—most valuable of all—encouragement during the composition of this book. This is my small opportunity to recognize them and to offer thanks once more for all the assistance they gave me.

Clint Caddell of Pi-Tech in Granbury, Texas, was my support system for computer hardware, assembling my latest computer and answering my cries for help whenever disaster struck. Even more important, he introduced me to the high-resolution graphics software that made possible the construction of the maps in this book. His patience with my fumbling questions will always be remembered gratefully.

Dennis Beck of Fort Worth tolerated and inspired me in his continuous writing class at Texas Christian University. His critique of my first draft was penetrating and immensely helpful. Having moved from the Fort Worth area, I miss those Thursday evening workshops that were so helpful and so filled with good humor.

Becky Harris gamely transcribed hours of audiotapes and from my dictation produced a readable text.

Katherine ("Kit") Goodwin of the University of Texas at Arlington was most helpful in locating pertinent maps, data, and other surprising material. Her clues led me to sources that filled in large gaps in my information.

Loren Wilson read my early manuscript and offered timely suggestions. By constantly inquiring about the status of this book, he provided a strong stimulus for me to stay at the word processor and complete the project.

Malcolm Coon of MC Squared in San Antonio played a key role in printing the county maps from my computer disks. High-resolution printing was required to make the maps camera-ready for the publisher. A long search for the computer-printer combination capable of accomplishing this task led repeatedly to dead ends. One shop with the requisite capacity disappeared from the face of the earth—taking with it with some of my computer disks. Promptly and with a high degree of expertise, Malcolm and his staff produced the excellent set of county maps presented in this book.

Dr. Don Dyal, head of Special Collections in the Texas A&M University Library, carefully reviewed my manuscript. He not only offered helpful suggestions, but also found some mischievous errors that, but for him, would have proved most embarrassing.

Last but never least, I thank my wife, Alys, for her backing, patience, and understanding during the long periods when I was immersed in dusty history books and crumbling maps. She also served as a special editor who helped me cope with a multitude of grammatical pitfalls.

TEXAS BOUNDARIES

1 · Early Maps of Texas

Early Explorers

The map of Texas had its beginning on June 2, 1519, when a Spanish explorer named Alonzo Álvarez de Piñeda sailed westward from Florida down the entire coast of Texas. The governor of Jamaica had outfitted him with four ships and a crew of 270 men, and had commissioned him to map the coastline to the north. Members of the crew drew a sketch of the coastline, but no record exists indicating that they came ashore. This sketch, now known as Piñeda's map, is reproduced as map 1-1.[1]

One can discern prominent features in Piñeda's map. Cuba and the peninsulas of Florida and Yucatan are unmistakable, as are the mouths of major rivers. Despite the primitive nature of ocean navigation in 1519, Piñeda's placement of these and other features is remarkable.

Piñeda's map was the first ever made of the Gulf Coast. It is also the oldest recorded document of Texas history.

On November 6, 1528, a shipwrecked Spaniard, Álvar Núñez, Cabeza de Vaca, became probably the first foreigner to set foot on what is now Texas. His ordeals and wanderings are well known to readers of Texas history.[2] Although he was without instruments and could only dead reckon his way back to Mexico, his recollections of rivers, plant life, landforms, and Native Americans furnished a picture enticing to future explorers. De Vaca traveled in the company of three other survivors: the Spaniards Alonso del Castillo and Andrés Dorantes and a Moor named Estevancio. (Moors were prohibited from traveling to New Spain at the time, and Estevancio had probably stowed away on the ship from Spain.) These four recounted their experiences in a joint report that included as much geographical information as they could reconstruct. Their verbal map left much to be desired,

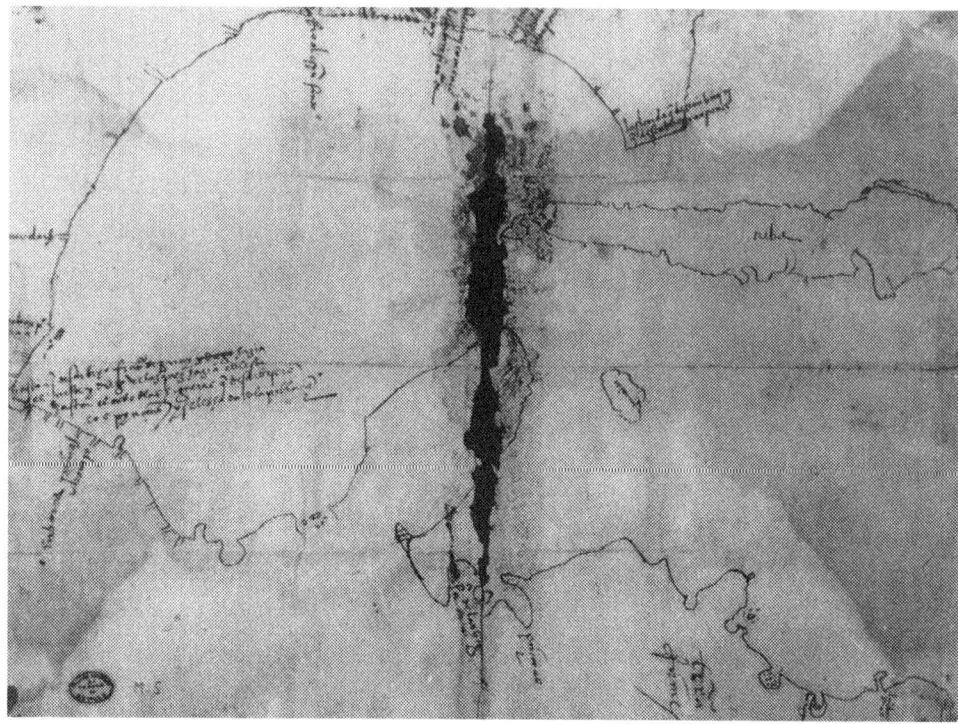

MAP 1-1. Piñeda's 1519 map of the Texas Gulf Coast, drawn on a sailing trip from Florida to Lower Mexico. Map reproduced from the collections of the Barker Texas History Center, University of Texas at Austin.

and scholars still hotly debate the route taken by these wanderers. However, their description did document the abundant presence of rivers and streams in Texas, as well as demonstrating that it was possible to travel into New Spain by land from a point near the mouth of the Mississippi River.

Piñeda and de Vaca soon were followed by Francisco Vásquez de Coronado (1540) and Luis de Moscoso de Alvarado (1542). While searching in vain for de Vaca's mystical Seven Cities of Cibola, Coronado unwittingly became a geographer and mapped a path from the Rio Grande to the Grand Canyon, then northeastward into what is now Kansas. As rewards, Coronado received a head injury falling from a horse and a demotion upon his return to Mexico.

One of Coronado's columns reached into present East Texas and met a group of Caddoan Indians, a branch of the Hasinai Confederacy. This confederacy was composed of culturally related East Texas tribes and included the Anadarko, Natchitoch, Nabedache, Nasoni, Hainai, Amediche, Adaes, Nacono, Neche, and Nacogdoche.

Shortly after this brief venture into East Texas by some of Coronado's men, another group of Spaniards approached this area from the east. Hernando de Soto came from Florida with six hundred men and traversed most of the Southeast in search of riches. Nearing his death on the banks of the Mississippi River, de Soto passed his command to Moscoso, who set out to find an overland route into New Spain.

Along the way, Moscoso met the friendly Caddoan Indians and observed that they greeted each other with a word he understood to be *Tejas*. To the Caddoans, this word phonetically was more like *Teychas* and probably meant *friend* or *ally*, but it became the Spanish name for all Indians of the Hasinai Confederacy. When documenting these reports in Castilian Spanish, translators preferred an easier pronunciation and substituted an *x* for the *j*. Thereafter, the tribe and then the entire area became known as *Texas*.

The Spaniards had planned to designate the new area *New Philippines* after King Philip II. Had it not been for Moscoso's encounter with the Caddoans and the translators' errors, the residents of Texas—and not those of a Pacific island nation—today would be called Filipinos.

Moscoso became discouraged and did not reach Mexico by land as he had intended. He traveled into what is now Texas, probably as far as the Trinity River in Houston County before turning back toward the Mississippi. His maps contained errors, and exact routes are questionable, but there is no doubt that he crossed the Red, Sabine, and Angelina rivers. Had he been a better mapmaker, there might be less debate over his routes.

The paths taken by these three explorers is a controversial subject among historians. Chipman thoroughly researched this issue,[3] embodying his conclusions in our map 1-2. This map displays probable routes for the first three groups who explored Texas. Of course, the towns shown did not exist at the time but are provided for reference.

Information developed by Coronado, Moscoso, and Cabeza de Vaca produced a rudimentary picture of Texas. They recorded rivers, creeks, ridges, hills, and plant and animal life. One or another of them crossed every major river in the future state; thus they became the first to map the interior of Texas.

Information on the approximate size and location of topographical features was valuable to future travelers in this new land and served the Spanish government well in the establishment of presidios (forts) and missions. As settlers later moved into the province and began to define landholdings, these natural features became the first landmarks of ownership. In the early 1800s, when the Mexican government devised municipalities as a form of local government, these same topographical features, especially rivers and their tributaries, frequently were cited as boundaries. This tradition held; even today, many county boundary definitions employ such markers.

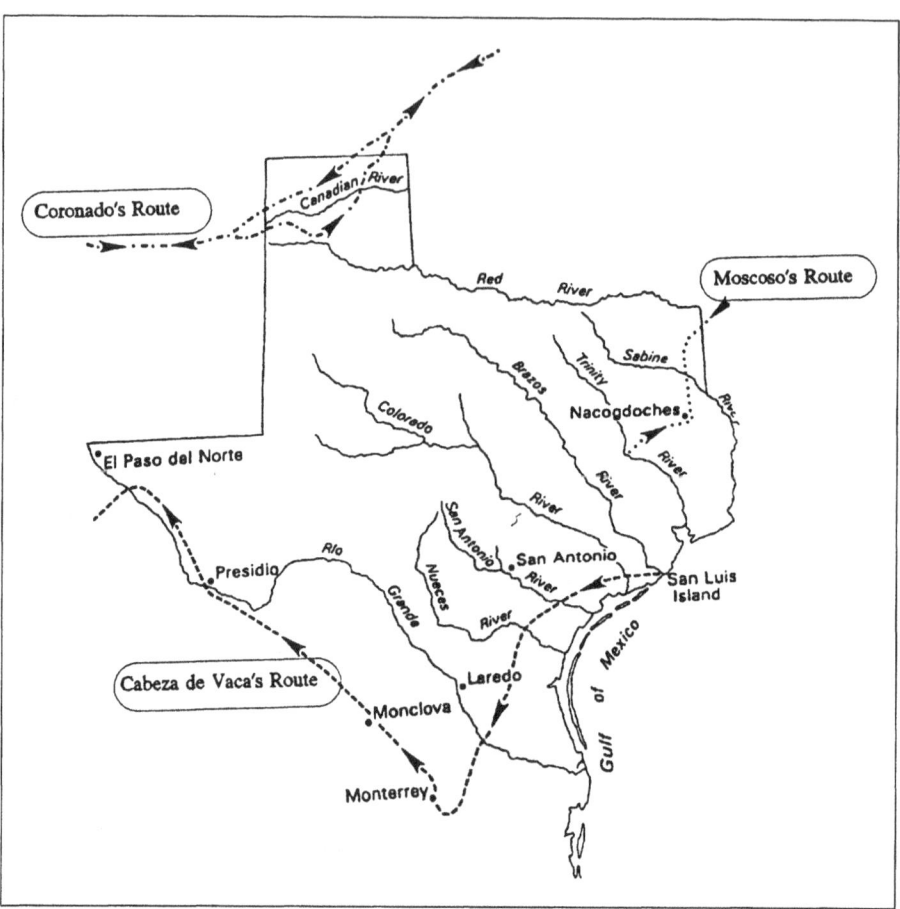

MAP 1-2. Probable routes of de Vaca (1528), Coronado (1540), and Moscoso (1542). Adapted from Donald E. Chipman, *Spanish Texas, 1519–1821* (Austin: University of Texas Press, 1992). Used by permission of the University of Texas Press.

Government by the Spanish

Faced with the necessity of governing colonies in New Spain, the Spanish rulers transplanted their political forms and customs without alteration. At the pinnacle of the Spanish hierarchy was the king, an absolute monarch, who appointed a Council of the Indies specifically to supervise and administer emigration to the New World. Unfortunately, this council never left Spain to examine the New World and so had no firsthand knowledge of the subjects or the land.

As the foreign colonies grew, they demanded more attention, and a viceroyalty was created in 1535, encompassing all the territory from Panama to Oregon. The king appointed a viceroy, who was the chief government official of this area and who answered directly to the king. The viceroy was first in command and resided in New Spain.

Under the viceroy, a captain general was supposed to assist in administering outlying districts. But, as often as not, this official went his own way, bypassing the viceroy and speaking directly with the Council of the Indies in Spain. Not infrequently, he went straight to the king. These conflicting lines of authority helped make colonial government sluggish and so caused delays in settling areas north of the Rio Grande.

Judicial matters were meant to be handled by the Audiencia. Judges, prosecuting attorneys, and other officials comprised this nebulous body whose structure was never made clear. Complications frequently arose because of the loosely defined court system.

Colonists who came to Texas under Spanish rule all came under the sway of these governmental systems. To most such settlers, this form of government seemed alien, and they discarded it after Texas became a republic.

The modern county government of Texas is based upon this early Spanish, and later Mexican, pattern. But the first Texas Constitution, in its details, reflected new Anglo-American concepts.

For over three hundred years, both Texas and Mexico were part of New Spain and hence came under the jurisdiction of the viceroy. As population increased, the viceroyalty, as a method of government, became untenable; in 1776, Spain was obliged to create political subdivisions called states. One group of states, designated the Eastern Internal Provinces, included Texas, Coahuila, Nuevo León, Nuevo Santander, and Tamaulipas.

The question of the eastern boundary of Texas is not new to historians and has spawned countless graduate theses, publications, and books. This boundary figured prominently in the contest between Spain and France for control of the Southwest.

Spain regarded as hers the western regions of Louisiana and in 1716 established the community of Los Adaes near what today is Robeline, Louisiana.[4] Los Adaes was the colonial capital of Spanish Texas from 1721 to 1773. It hosted the mission San Miguel de los Adaes and the presidio Nuestra Señora del Pilar de los Adaes. Spain's intent was to check French expansion toward Texas. France protested Los Adaes mightily, but in fact both countries benefited from the settlement. Los Adaes existed for fifty years as a center of trade, a diplomatic exchange post, and a port for exchange of contraband. When France ceded Louisiana to Spain in 1762, Los Adaes no longer was needed and was abandoned by the Spanish government, which then moved the colonial capital to San Antonio de Bexar.

Louisiana was re-ceded to France in 1800, and Napoleon sold the vast area to the United States in 1803.

The new boundary between Spain and the United States was vague;

MAP 1-3. The 1903 Louisiana Purchase from France. Boundaries, shown in bold lines, were defined largely by rivers and drainage patterns. Zones of potential boundary conflict are evident. Map by Luke Gournay.

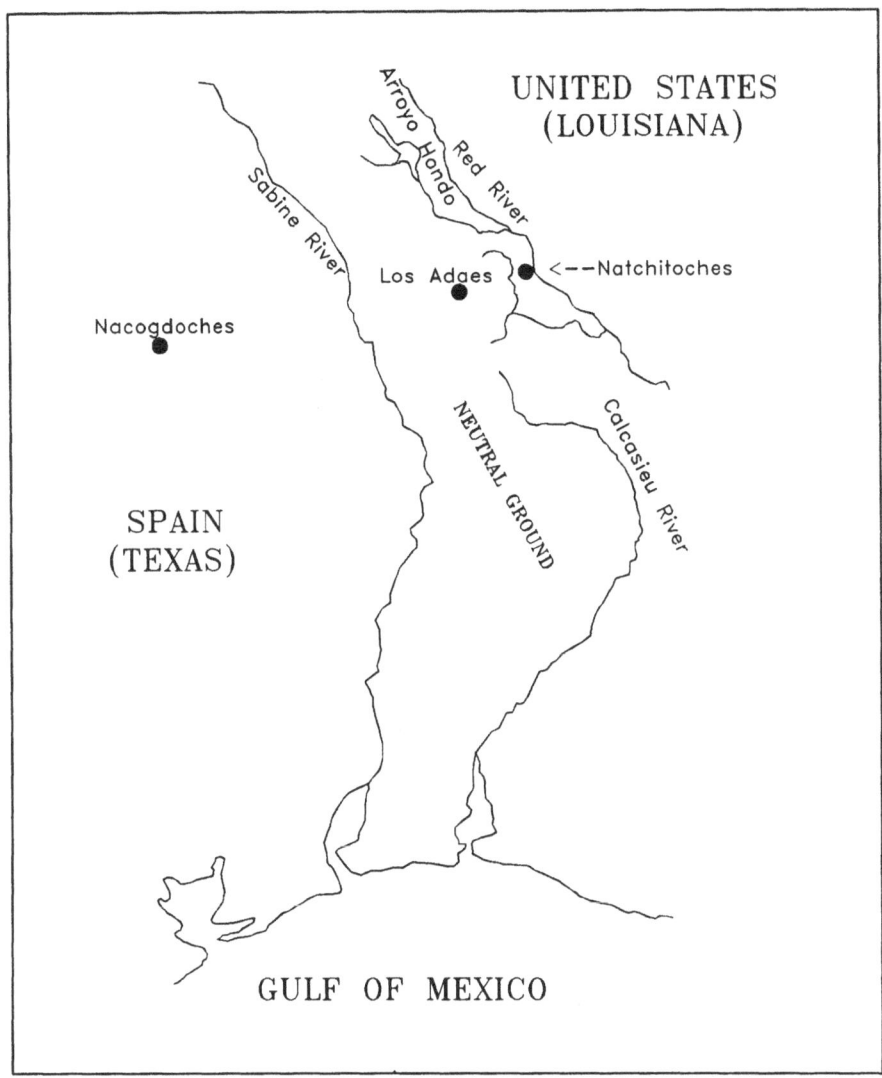

MAP 1-4. Neutral territory agreed to by the United States and Spain in 1806, to avoid a territorial war. Map by Luke Gournay.

some say Napoleon purposely made it so for his own devious reasons. Map 1-3 gives the approximate bounds of the purchase and shows some overlap in ownership claims.

Contention over territory began immediately, initiating a threat of war between the two countries. To avert armed conflict, the United States and Spain established a neutral zone between the Sabine River on the west and the Arroyo Hondo and Calcasieu rivers on the east.[5] This zone is depicted

MAP 1-5. Boundaries between Spain and the United States established in 1819 by the Adams-Oñís Treaty. This treaty clarified the eastern boundary of Texas. Map by Luke Gournay.

in map 1-4. While diplomatic haggling proceeded toward a solution, this zone remained bereft of government, and those elements which thrive on anarchy soon occupied it. It was decades after a boundary settlement before this area was brought under civil control.

Finally, in 1819, John Quincy Adams, the American secretary of state, and

Don Luis de Oñís y Gonzales, the Spanish minister to the United States, agreed on the western boundary of the United States and, consequently, on the eastern boundary of Texas. Their settlement, known as the Adams-Oñís Treaty, is pictured in map 1-5. Years later, Texas, with some success, used elements of this map to claim territory as far north as Wyoming.

The question of boundaries between Spain (and Texas) and the United States nominally went uncontested during the remainder of Spanish rule. Disputes flared again after Mexico became independent and the Texans fought for their own freedom.

Notes

1. The original map rests in the Spanish Historical Archives, Archivo General de Indias, Seville, Spain: Mapas y Planos, México 5. The map has been reproduced recently in Donald E. Chipman, *Spanish Texas, 1519–1821* (Austin: University of Texas Press, 1992), 24; and in Robert S. Martin and James C. Martin, *Contours of Discovery: Printed Maps Delineating the Texas and Southwestern Chapters in the Cartographic History of North America, 1513–1930* (Austin: Texas State Historical Association, 1982), 11. A copy of the map is in the Barker Texas History Center, University of Texas, Austin.

2. Numerous descriptions of de Vaca's experiences exist. Some are: Fanny Bandelier, trans., *The Journey of Álvar Núñez, Cabeza de Vaca, and His Companions from Florida to the Pacific, 1528–1536*, edited by Ad. F. Bandelier (New York: Allerton Book Company, 1922); Herbert Davenport and Joseph K. Wells, "The First Europeans in Texas, 1528–36" *Southwestern Historical Quarterly* 22, no. 2 (October, 1918): 111–42, no. 3 (January, 1919): 205–59; Cleve Hallenbeck, *Álvar Núñez, Cabeza de Vaca: The Journey and Route of the First Europeans to Cross the Continent of North America, 1534–1535* (Glendale, Calif.: Arthur H. Clark Company, 1940); Theodore H. Lewis, ed. "The Narrative of Álvar Núñez Cabeza de Vaca," *Spanish Exploration in the Southern United States, 1528–1543* (New York: Charles Scribner's Sons, 1925).

3. Chipman, *Spanish Texas*, 31.

4. T. R. Fehrenbach, *Lone Star: A History of Texas and the Texans* (New York: American Legacy Press, 1983).

5. Walter P. Webb and H. Bailey Carroll, eds., *The Handbook of Texas* (Austin: Texas State Historical Association, 1952).

2 · The Colonial Period and Texas Land Grants

The Spaniards' quest for immense gold and silver deposits in Texas proved fruitless. Instead, they found enormous expanses of land and countless Indians, some of them hostile. With the discovery of French activities along the Sabine and Neches rivers, the Spanish became obsessed with the possibility of French intrusion into the Texas part of New Spain. This worry dominated Spanish policies toward the new realm during all of Spain's time in power.

In order to gain and maintain control of this territory, Spain needed to settle upon it a large and industrious population. Despite the intentions of the Spanish government, this goal remained beyond reach. For the residents of New Spain, the risks of moving to the frontier were great; conditions were harsh, and the constant threat of Indian predation made life precarious. The people in the interior of New Spain were comfortable and secure, and they had no convincing incentives to venture into this formidable territory.

In 1719, the Spanish Council of the Indies saw that a new initiative was necessary to populate the province of Texas. It proposed that two hundred families should be recruited from the Canary Islands off the coast of West Africa, from Galicia in Spain, or from Havana, Cuba, and settled in Texas. But under Spanish rule, the wheels of the bureaucracy ground slowly. Twelve years passed before fifteen families, a total of fifty-six persons, arrived at San Antonio de Bexar from the Canary Islands. Known as *Isleños*, they applied themselves mainly to farming and so often found themselves at odds with the earlier Spanish settlers, the *Bexareños*, who were cattle ranchers.

Despite their initial differences, the two groups eventually merged, ethnically and politically. Together, they founded the first civilian settlement, Villa San Fernando de Bexar, a community which was to become the leading town in Spanish Texas. By 1743, they were jointly electing and appointing magistrates and representatives to supervise their community. Today, several San Antonio residents trace their lineages back to the Isleños of this epoch.

During the rest of the sixteenth century, the Spaniards concentrated on founding missions and constructing military forts, commonly called *presidios*. The few efforts made to expand the population were ineffective, and the end of the century saw fewer than five thousand persons of European heritage in the region.

Only forty years after the United States colonies revolted and gained their independence from England, Americans and Europeans were pushing westward against the Spanish borders of Texas. By the early nineteenth century, settlers were moving illegally past the Sabine River from Louisiana and into the rich lands of East Texas.

After a period of reluctance and vacillation, the Spanish government accepted the inevitable and legalized this movement, putting aside its fear of foreigners. The Spaniards made land grants to American and European empresarios but hoped to retain tight control of Texas. Although severe stipulations governed ownership, one could never be entirely certain of holding legal title to land. To acquire land, a person had to become a Roman Catholic and promise that a Catholic priest would perform all marriages. Additional rules and taxes followed.

Moses Austin and his son obtained the first Spanish land grants. Maps of the Austins' grants and those that followed served as preludes to the maps that depicted Texas after it gained independence. Within—and sometimes coterminous with—these grants, municipalities were formed as governmental units that later became counties.

Gen. Joaquín de Arredondo, chief civil and military commander of Texas, approved the first grant on January 17, 1821. It went to Moses Austin, a Connecticut-born entrepreneur, but Moses became ill with pneumonia and died before he could develop a colony. The grant and the challenge were passed to his son, Stephen F. Austin, a well-educated man suited for leadership. However, a year passed before Stephen Austin could satisfy the Mexican bureaucracy and bring in the first settlers. During this time, Mexico was in revolt against Spanish rule, and internally a state of great confusion existed. Austin later obtained a second smaller grant and then, in partnership with Samuel May Williams, a third grant.

The new Mexican government at various times questioned the validity of the Spanish grants; as late as 1836, its position regarding new grants had not solidified.

Nevertheless, when Mexican rule ended in 1836, a large number of grants existed in Texas. Records were unclear as to which grants truly had been sanctioned by either the Spanish or the Mexican government. Such legal questions, however, did not slow the printers, who busied themselves drawing and distributing a colorful assortment of maps. The main purpose of the maps was to induce the adventurous to move to Texas; geographical accuracy was not a prime consideration.

Of the maps published around 1836, only three are consistent with each other. One is attributed to David H. Burr and was published in 1833 by J. H. Colton and Company of New York. Another was compiled by Stephen F. Austin and published by H. S. Tanner of Philadelphia in 1835. The third was drawn by E. F. Lee and published by J. A. James and Company in 1836. Additionally, detailed written descriptions of grant boundaries are given in Barker's treatise on Texas history.[1]

Information gleaned from these three maps and data from Barker's treatise were collated to form the most probable picture of Texas in 1836. Map 2-1 represents these merged data.

Stephen F. Austin's was the first and the largest colony in Texas. It extended along the coast of the Gulf of Mexico from Galveston Bay to Matagorda Bay and then inland to the Old San Antonio Road, which ran through today's Burleson and Lee counties. Austin's was undoubtedly the best organized and most successful empresario operation in Texas. His accomplishments were made under conditions more trying than those facing the first English colonists on the Atlantic coast. He is universally regarded as the Father of Texas.

Green C. DeWitt, on April 15, 1825, obtained an empresario grant to settle four hundred families. His land generally lay south of, and adjacent to, Austin's. Problems immediately arose because of faulty maps. The description of DeWitt's land placed it in the "region south of the Old San Antonio Road, between the Lavaca River and the divide separating the Guadalupe and San Antonio Rivers." This vague wording created conflict with Martín de León, whose 1824 grant seemed to overlap DeWitt's. With such vague descriptions, it is small wonder that strife became constant. With the dispute temporarily in abeyance, however, DeWitt's people settled the town of Gonzales and adjacent communities. A Mexican law of 1830 restricting immigration did not staunch the flow of settlers into the DeWitt grant area; by the end of that year, the colony was well populated and prosperous.

Map 2-1 incorporates a version of Wavell and Milam's grant in northeastern Texas between the Red and the Sabine rivers. Both Ben Milam and A. G. Wavell worked at obtaining this land, and their application for a grant was approved on March 9, 1826.[2] Ownership immediately became clouded when the United States claimed that the land lay east of the boundary

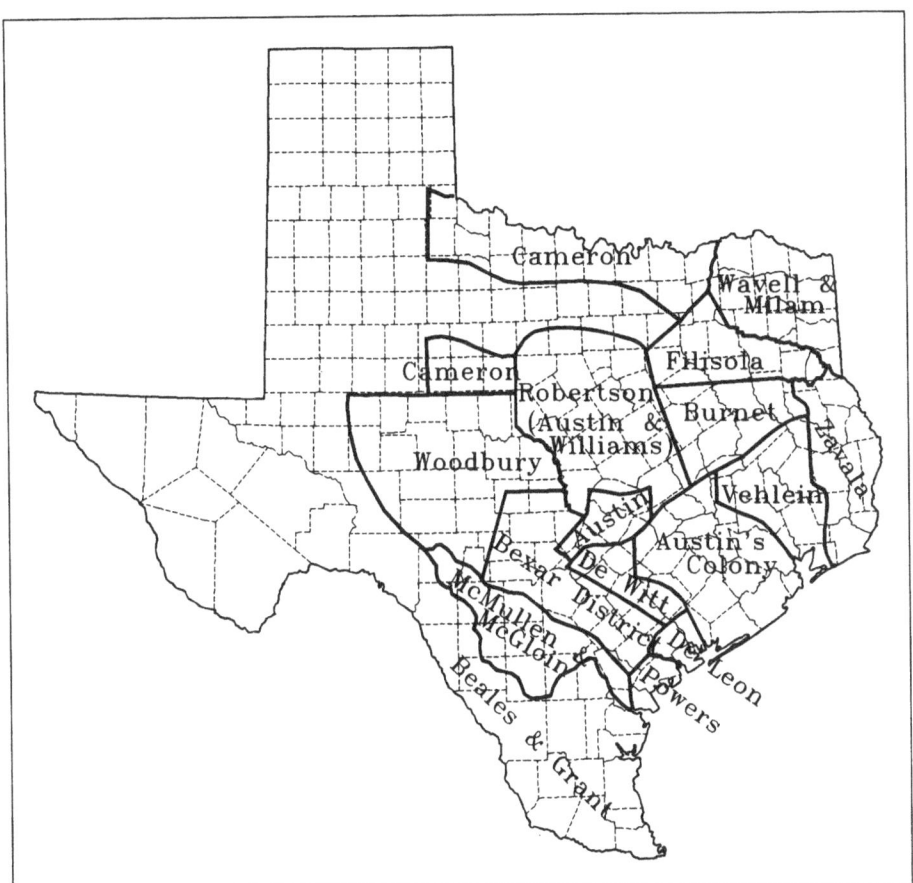

MAP 2-I. The land grants in Texas as of 1835. Map by Luke Gournay.

established with Mexico in 1819 and therefore did not form part of Texas. Wavell continued efforts to establish his claims with the Republic of Texas and later with the State of Texas, but he never was successful.

The grant that generated the greatest dispute by far was that of Austin and Williams, also known as the Robertson Grant.[3] This grant originated with the Texas Association of Nashville, Tennessee, when Robert Leftwich in 1825 obtained a contract to settle eight hundred families in Texas. The area, about one hundred miles wide and two hundred miles long, encompassed all or part of thirty present counties.

Having opened the gates to immigration, Mexico became concerned over the large influx of foreigners. As settlers streamed in, Mexico passed a law in 1830 that stopped all immigration except to colonies where at least one hundred families had already settled.

By 1830, Sterling C. Robertson was the Nashville company agent, and this new Mexican law could have spelled disaster for him and his colony. Stephen F. Austin and his agent Samuel M. Williams tried to take advantage of this situation by applying for a contract on land that overlapped the Robertson project. Publicly they justified their action by claiming that the Mexicans would not let the Nashville company continue to operate. Privately they reasoned that they might as well move in and secure a northern buffer for the Austin colony. But Robertson had already settled over one hundred families, and he fought for what he felt was rightfully his. He presented his evidence to the Mexican authorities and prevailed. In May 1834, the governor of Coahuila and Texas annulled the Austin-Williams contract and restored Robertson's contract. The empresario title came to Robertson, and the territory became known as the Robertson Colony.

But that was not to be the end of the issue. In 1835, Williams persisted and convinced the governor to rescind his decision favoring Robertson. Before Robertson could mount another defensive battle, the revolt against Mexico began, and the Texas Constitution replaced Mexican laws and rules. Under Robertson's leadership, over six hundred families settled in the colony.

A consequence of these exchanges was a long litany of land disputes that continued for decades. Typically, both empresarios gave titles to one tract of land, setting the stage for interminable litigation.

Near the end of the colonial period, an area roughly corresponding to Robertson's Colony became a municipality named Viesca. Its name was changed to Milam by the Provisional Government in 1835, and Milam emerged as one of the original counties in 1836.

The McMullen-McGloin Colony[4] was founded in 1828 by two Irishmen, John McMullen and James McGloin. The colony originally was called San Patricio Hibernia after the Irish patron saint, but the settlers soon shortened the name by dropping Hibernia. The (mostly Irish) colonists from New York obtained a total of eighty-four land titles before the Texas Revolution began.

John Lucius Woodbury received an empresario contract from the Mexican government in 1826 to settle two hundred families in Texas. There is no evidence that Woodbury brought in any families or made any move to fulfill his contract.

Don Martín de León[5] obtained an empresario grant in 1824, with authority to settle Mexican families in Texas. As a Catholic and a Mexican citizen with a fine reputation and good finances, he received special considerations not generally extended to European applicants. De León founded his first town on the Guadalupe River and named it Guadalupe Victoria. By 1833, the village numbered over two hundred people, most Mexicans but some from Ireland and the United States. The citizens were eager participants in the formation of a new independent government. They attended the Consultation of 1835, a meeting of colonists held to decide what position to take regarding the Mexican restrictions. They also attended and supported the Convention of 1836 which posited a revolt from Mexico. Their representatives signed the Texas Declaration of Independence at this convention and a contingent of volunteers fought in the revolution. Their support of the revolutionaries proved a double-edged sword. As the Mexican army advanced in March 1836, it considered the colonists traitors and treated them accordingly. Then, after Sam Houston's victory at San Jacinto, components of his army poured into Victoria and ravaged the colony. These soldiers labeled the residents enemy aliens and confiscated some of their lands and other possessions. They established a new municipal government, removing all Mexicans from office and substituting Anglos. In spite of these setbacks, some colonists weathered the storm, and their progeny live in the area today.

David G. Burnet, Lorenzo de Zavala, and Joseph Vehlein obtained separate empresario contracts for tracts of land in East Texas. Unable financially to manage a colony, they sold the title to their land on October 16, 1830, to the Galveston Bay and Texas Land Company. In what became a nightmarish fiasco, the company brought immigrants from Germany and Switzerland via New York. Upon sailing from New York to Texas, they found that the 1830 Mexican ban on immigration left them stranded at the mouth of the Trinity River. Here, they were permitted to build huts and plant gardens, but they could not obtain land titles.

Several agents represented the company over the next few years and lawsuits were filed, but nothing positive ever emerged from the project. The destitute immigrants, trapped in the debacle, suffered ruinous consequences and gradually merged into the existing population.

James Power and James Hewetson, both from Ireland, became partners and applied for empresario grants in 1825 to colonize along the Texas coast north of the Nueces River. Although their application was granted with modifications, it conflicted with those of de León and McMullen-McGloin. In this rare case, reason prevailed, and the parties reached a solution by compromise. The Irish immigrants suffered severe casualties due to cholera, but the survivors prospered and built a strong colony.

John Charles Beales and James Grant in 1832 acquired two grants that obligated them to settle eight hundred families in the region shown on map 2-1. Hardy immigrants from the United States, Spain, Germany, and England settled in that rocky, arid region between the Rio Grande and Nueces rivers. They built houses, started crops, and instituted a government; they would have done well, had the elements and circumstances not conspired against them. A severe drought, Santa Anna's invading army, and marauding Comanches brought an untimely end to a courageous group of people.

Cameron, Felisola, and Woodbury did not fulfill the requirements of their grants and let them lapse. Several other grantees did not attempt to colonize, and their land returned to the Mexican government. These grantees were: Richard Exeter and Stephen J. Wilson, Col. Juan Domínguez, Juan Antonio Padillo and Thomas J. Chambers, Frost Thorn, John G. Purnell and Benjamin Drake Lovell, J. C. Beales and José Manuel Royuela, and Juan Vicente Campos.

Most published maps misspelled the names of the empresarios Vehlein as Whelin, McGloin as McGlone, and Zavala as Zavalla. Other maps that appeared at the time must be viewed as mere interpretations and probably never reflected legal realities. Given poor to nonexistent surveying methods and deplorable record keeping, controversy surrounded most of the land grants. Debates over the ownership and the boundaries of land granted by Spanish and Mexican governments plagued the new Republic of Texas and persist even today.

Notes

1. Barker, Eugene C., *Readings in Texas History* (Dallas, Tex.: Southwest Press, 1929).
2. Walter P. Webb and H. Bailey Carroll, eds., *The Handbook of Texas* (Austin: Texas State Historical Association, 1952).
3. Richard Denny Parker, *Historical Recollections of Robertson County, Texas* (Salado, Tex.: Anson Jones Press, 1955).
4. William Herman Oberste, *Texas Irish Empresarios* (Austin: Von Boeckmann-Jones Co., 1953).
5. Victor M. Rose, *Settlement of Victoria, Texas* (Laredo, Tex.: Daily Times Print, 1898); republished as *Victor Rose's History of Victoria* (Victoria, Tex.: Book Mart, 1961).

3 · Mexican Government and Texas Boundaries

Mexico gained independence from Spain in 1821, after years of political and military strife. Not long afterward, on May 9, 1824, the Mexican Congress combined the states of Texas and Coahuila for governmental purposes. The Congress clearly specified that Texas would become a separate state when its population was large enough to warrant a separate government. This political linkage with Coahuila caused much dissension among the Texas colonists. They naturally wanted a center of government closer than Saltillo, a city in the interior of Mexico. The Mexican government's refusal to create a separate state government became a contributing cause of the Texas Revolution.

Map 3-1, a map of the combined states of Texas and Coahuila, along with neighboring states, suggests the distance from settlements in Texas to Saltillo.[1]

The Congress of Coahuila and Texas sought to ameliorate the situation by creating the Department of Bexar on August 15, 1824, with San Antonio de Bexar designated as capital of the department. Though still part of the state of Coahuila and Texas, the department included all of Texas and was created to serve the needs of Stephen Austin and the other colonists. The political head of the department was nominated by the local municipalities but appointed by the state governor for a four-year term.

Out of Bexar, the Congress in January 1831 created another department, Nacogdoches. This department comprised the eastern part of Texas and had its capital at Nacogdoches.

A third and final department, Brazos, was formed in March 1834. Situ-

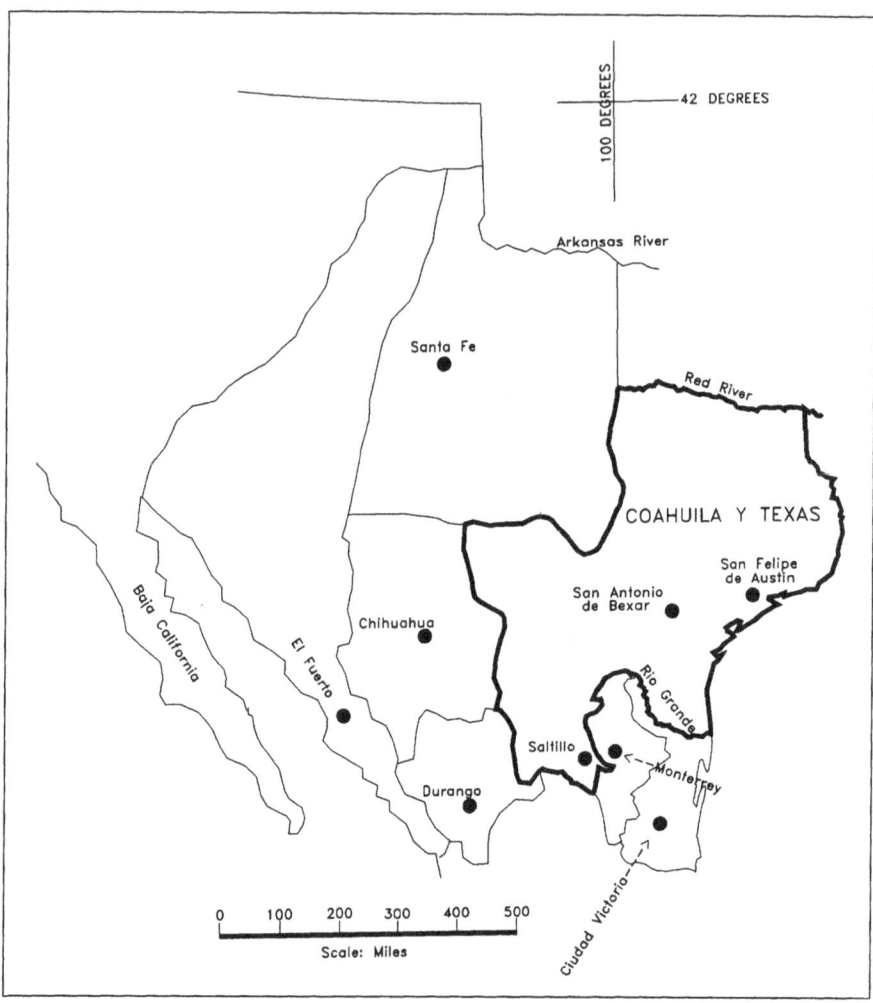

MAP 3-1. Texas, merged with Coahuila, in 1824. This merger was one of the issues that led to the Texas Revolution. Adapted from A. Ray Stephens and William M. Holmes, *Historical Atlas of Texas* (Norman: University of Oklahoma Press, 1989).

ated between the departments of Bexar and Nacogdoches, it had its capital at San Felipe de Austin.

These three departments, shown in map 3-2, made up the province of Texas in 1831.

Of particular significance is the fact that the Trans-Nueces area was not included within the boundaries of the province. Mexico recognized the Nueces River as the southern boundary of the Department of Bexar and the western boundary of the province of Texas. The Mexican state of Tamaulipas began at the Nueces River and extended southward.

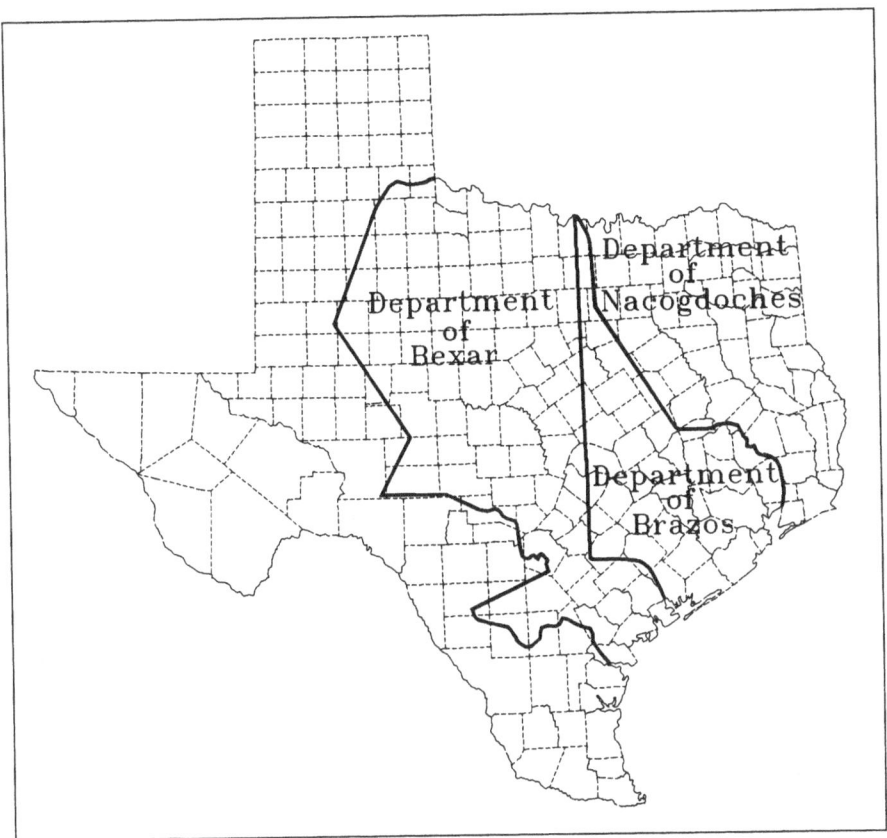

MAP 3-2. The three departments of the Province of Texas under Mexican rule in 1831. The Province of Texas was part of the Mexican State of Texas and Coahuila. Map by Luke Gournay.

Although Texans regarded the Trans-Nueces territory as their own after the revolt against Mexico, departmental maps do not support this claim. It was only after the Mexican-American War that the Treaty of Guadalupe-Hidalgo (1848) settled this issue.

Texas counties had their beginning in April 1832. Then, the Mexican legislature provided for the creation of municipalities with powers of local government.[2] At the urging of the Texas delegation, the Mexicans allowed the election of officers by popular vote of the residents.

This move was important for the Texans and represented another step in a process of decentralization by which the people distanced themselves from a national government. But it was a continuing disappointment to Texans that Mexico did not organize Texas as a separate state; instead, it remained linked governmentally with Coahuila.

The general structure of the Mexican *municipio* (municipality) closely resembled that established earlier by the Spanish. The largest local entity was the *ayuntamiento*, the governing body of a municipality.[3] A municipality encompassed not only a town but also the surrounding territory that fed people or goods into the town. The *ayuntamiento* resembled our modern city council or commissioners court and was charged with providing for law and order, roads and bridges, and the health and education of the municipality's residents.

The reigning figure of the *ayuntamiento* was the *alcalde*.[4] He acted as mayor, judge, and leading citizen. Sharing duties with him were two to four *regidores* (our county commissioners or city council members). A *síndico procurador* acted as prosecuting attorney.

Municipalities had subdivisions known as precincts. Each of these was presided over by a *comisario* or *subalcalde*, whose office evolved into that of the modern justice of the peace. The office of *alguacil* was formed to encompass the duties of today's sheriff.

By 1835, twelve Texas municipalities were functioning under the rules established by the Mexican Constitution. They were: Austin, Bevil, Columbia, Gonzales, Harrisburg, Liberty, Matagorda, Mina, Nacogdoches, San Augustine, Viesca, and Washington.

Increasing friction between the colonists and the Mexican government led to a historic meeting at San Felipe de Austin in October 1835. Representatives from the twelve municipalities attended and debated what attitude the Texans should take toward the Mexican dictatorship. Known as the Consultation, this group hastily prepared a document called the "Organic Law." Under the "Organic Law," the group unilaterally created a government for Texas as a separate state within the Mexican nation. From this date until a Constitution was drawn up in 1836, Texas ruled itself as a state with an organization called the General Council, or Provisional Government, as defined by the "Organic Law."

Although the Texans professed a desire to continue functioning as part of Mexico, their actions contravened the Mexican Constitution. The Texans' legal maneuver could only provoke Mexican retaliation.

Elected representatives from the municipalities made up the Provisional Government, and they elected an Anglo-American, Henry Smith, as state governor. These men moved away from the traditional Spanish influence, incorporating new concepts advocated by American colonists.

Through elaborate and dubious legal maneuvers, the Provisional Government created eleven new municipalities and changed the names of several others.

When the settlement of Bevil became a municipality in 1834, it was named after John Bevil, an early homesteader. In an exercise of dubious authority, the Texas Provisional Government honored William Jasper, of

American Revolution fame, by changing the name Bevil to Jasper in December 1835. Nothing in the "Organic Law" had granted the group authority to tinker with place names.

The Mexican government, on May 1, 1832, had formed the Municipality of Brazoria out of the Municipality of San Felipe (Austin) and named the town of Brazoria as municipal capital. In 1834, when some of Brazoria's territory was taken to form the Municipality of Matagorda, the names of both municipality and capital were changed from Brazoria to Columbia. The Provisional Government, again usurping authority, changed the name back to Brazoria.

Tenehaw (later Shelby) was the first new jurisdiction created on November 9, 1835. On this same day, a resolution was submitted to the Consultation that invited the settlers on Red River to join with the Consultation. The Red River contingent appeared at the convention on March 1, 1836, and accepted. With some question about its legality and greater questions about its location, the Provisional Government created the Municipality of Jefferson on November 13, 1835.

On November 16, Juan A. Padilla, a representative from Guadalupe-Victoria, presented his credentials and took a seat in the Provisional Government. James Power came from Refugio on November 22 and Ira Westover from Goliad the next day to join the government and represent their districts. Lewis Ayers' appearance on December 1, with credentials from San Patricio, brought the government of Texas to eighteen districts. The number increased to nineteen on December 5, when Provisional Governor Henry Smith approved an ordinance that created the Municipality of Jackson. Sabine and Colorado became municipalities on December 15, 1835, and January 8, 1836, respectively.

It was not until the convention assembled at Washington-on-the-Brazos on March 1, 1836, that representatives from Bexar and Red River arrived to join the emergent nation.

At this convention, twenty-three governmental districts voiced their declaration of independence from Mexico and wrote a document that proclaimed a new government for Texas.

The General Council had acted without any enabling authority to create eleven municipalities and to change the names of some. But no one contested their bold actions, and their assumption of authority was ratified by the Constitution of 1836.

In time, the twenty-three municipalities became known as counties and evolved into the two hundred fifty-four governmental entities of today.

Notes

1. A. Ray Stephens and William M. Holmes, *Historical Atlas of Texas* (Norman: University of Oklahoma Press, 1989).
2. Henderson Yoakum, *History of Texas from its First Settlement in 1685 to its annexation to the United States in 1846* (New York: Redfield, 1855; facsimile reproduction, Austin: Steck Company, 1935).
3. David Barnett Edward, *The History of Texas* (Cincinnati, Ohio: J. A. James, 1836; rptd. Austin: Texas State Historical Association, 1990).
4. Seymour V. Conner, "County Government in the Republic of Texas," *Southwestern Historical Quarterly* 55, no. 2 (October 1951): 163–200.

4 · First Boundaries of the Republic of Texas

The Republic of Texas, from its beginning, could and did claim to be larger than in fact it was. Boundary uncertainties among France, Spain, Mexico, and the United States set the stage for the newcomer to lay claim to lands on its borders.

The first Congress of Texas passed an act defining its boundaries. President Sam Houston approved the act on December 19, 1836, which read in part:

> the civil and political boundaries of this Republic be and is hereby declared to extend . . . Beginning at the mouth of the Sabine River and running west along the Gulf of Mexico, three leagues from land, to the mouth of the Rio Grande, thence up the principal stream of said river to its source, thence due north to the forty-second degree of north latitude, thence along the boundary line as defined in the treaty between the United States and Spain, to the beginning.[1]

This boundary included lands west of the Nueces River that Mexico claimed, lands that the United States claimed in the territories of Arkansas and Oklahoma, and an enormous stretch of land extending into present Wyoming. Map 4-1 reveals the scope of these claims. The brief discussion that follows focuses on those boundaries about which the greatest conflicts arose.

Major Boundary Disputes

For nearly three years after annexation to the United States, Texas quarreled with the national government over the state's western boundary. The Treaty of Guadalupe-Hidalgo explicitly stated that the western Texas boundary would be the Rio Grande from its mouth to its source. But after the Mexican-American War, United States soldiers controlled all the territory west of the one hundred-third meridian. Before becoming a state, Texas created Santa Fe County out of this vast area. The republic's action was pointless, for the federal troops prohibited the establishment of a judiciary body in the county seat of Santa Fe.

National officials ignored the Texas governor's protests concerning the occupation. At one point in 1849, Governor Wood, in a letter to the Texas Legislature, asked for all powers and resources of the state to oust the United States troops. Governor Bell, who followed him, threatened to take the area by force.

In another move to establish control, the Texas Legislature subdivided Santa Fe County into four counties—Santa Fe, Worth, El Paso, and Presidio. These are sketched in map 4-2.

The slavery issue entered the argument, northern United States senators spoke of dividing Texas into several states, and the state debt became linked with the problem. In consequence, only two years after annexation, Texas threatened to secede from the Union.

The two parties eventually reached a compromise. On November 25, 1850, Texas ceded the Upper Rio Grande to the United States in exchange for $10 million. Worth and Santa Fe counties ceased to exist; the northern limit of El Paso County was withdrawn to the present border with New Mexico.

THE TRANS-NUECES

Under Spain, the area between the Nueces and Rio Grande rivers long had been regarded as part of the states of Nuevo Santander and Coahuila. They called it *El Desierto Muerto*[2] because of its desolation; it was a no-man's-land occupied by bandits, freebooters, robbers, and angry Comanches. Guerrilla warfare raged between Texas and Mexico for ten years; Indians alternately supported one side and then the other, or sometimes both.

After the Treaty of Velasco with Santa Ana specified that the Mexican army would retreat beyond the Rio Grande, Texas took the Rio Grande, and not the Nueces, as its southern boundary. To the Mexican government, the treaty was a worthless piece of paper.

In an attempt to cement its claim, the Texas Congress in 1846 created

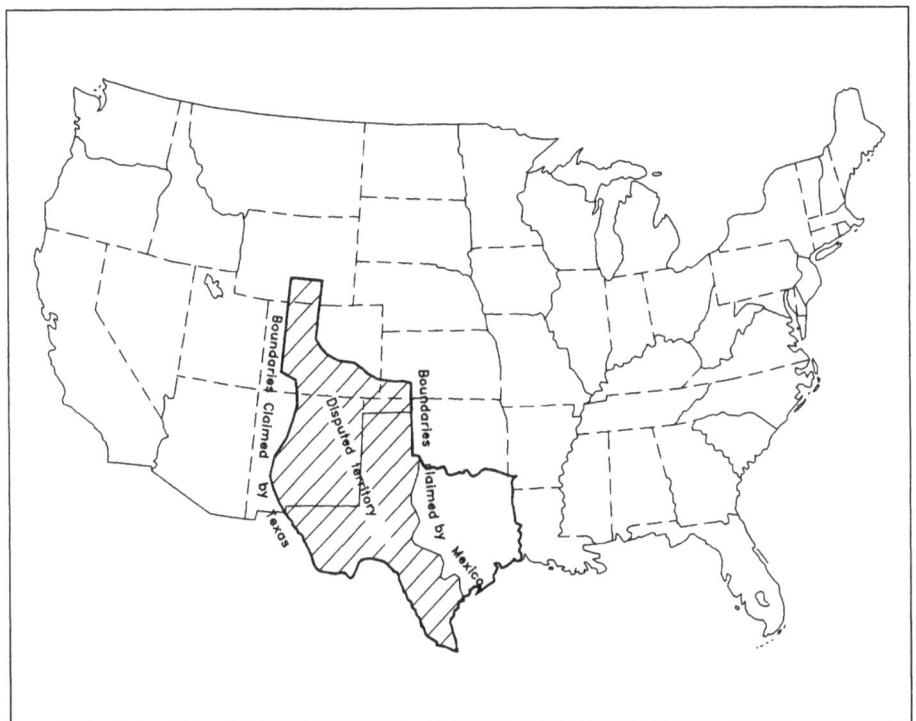

MAP 4-1. The territory claimed by Texas in its congressional act adopted on December 19, 1836. This territory included the hatched area plus the remainder of present Texas. Map by Luke Gournay.

Nueces County and established a county government at Corpus Christi. Nueces County filled the area between the Rio Grande and the Nueces rivers. The congress subdivided Nueces into Webb, Starr, and Cameron counties in 1848. This territorial argument ended with the Treaty of Guadalupe-Hidalgo after the Mexican-American War. By this treaty, Mexico renounced all claims to Texas and agreed that the Rio Grande, from its mouth to its source, would be the boundary.

This part of Texas remained untamed, and only in the late 1870s did dedicated efforts by the Texas Rangers bring a semblance of law and order to the "Nueces Strip."[3]

MILLER COUNTY

Another dispute arose in connection with the Arkansas border in the northeastern corner of Texas. The argument centered on Miller County. The Arkansas Territorial Legislature had created this large county in 1820; it included most of present Miller County, Arkansas, and the present Bowie,

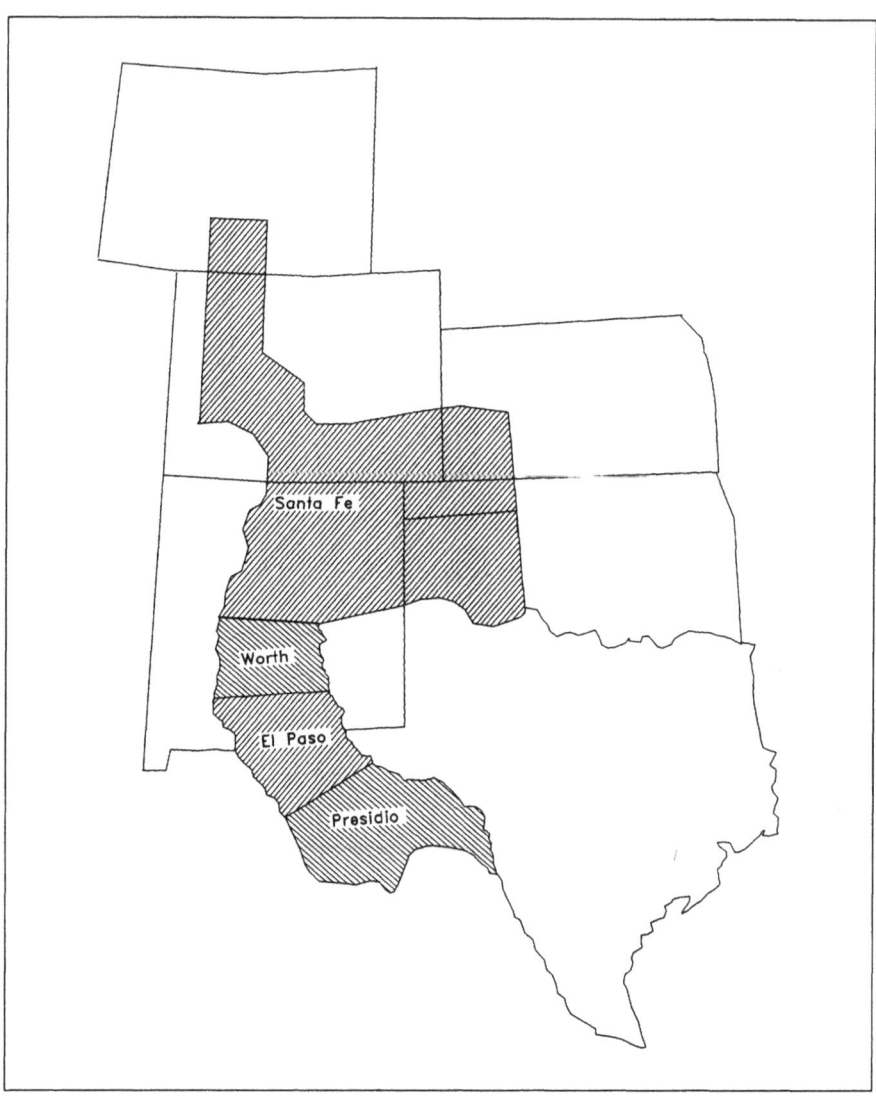

MAP 4-2. The division of Far West Texas into four counties: Santa Fe County in 1848, and El Paso, Worth, and Presidio counties in 1850. Map by Luke Gournay.

Cass, Delta, Fannin, Franklin, Hopkins, Hunt, Lamar, Morris, Red River, and Titus counties of Texas.

In one of its first acts, the Texas Congress took action to capture Miller County. It enacted a bill that provided for the first land office, Red River, and created Red River County. With enormous dimensions, the new county stretched east-west from present Texarkana to Wichita Falls and from the Red River to Longview in a north-south direction. This expanded Red

River County was larger than either Belgium or Holland; subsequent divisions turned it into all or part of twenty-eight Texas counties. It is drawn on map 5-2.

President Sam Houston vetoed the bill, largely because of the land office provision, but it passed over his veto in both houses on December 22, 1836.[4]

Insults flew back and forth between the Arkansans and the Texans until Texas became a state and the United States fixed the boundary at its present location.

GREER COUNTY

The state of Texas and the United States crossed swords in 1860, when the state legislature created Greer County with a north boundary that looped along the North Fork of the Red River instead of the South Fork. These features are drawn in map 5-19.

The Civil War delayed development of the county, but it was organized in 1886, with Mangum as county seat. The residents built a courthouse and jail, and two post offices and an extensive school system followed.

Citing the Adams-Oñís Treaty, erroneous maps, and an error in placing the one hundredth meridian, the United States claimed ownership of the county. State and federal attorneys argued this issue for many years, while Greer County continued to grow. The case finally reached the United States Supreme Court, which ruled in favor of the United States. On March 16, 1896, thirty-six years after its creation, Greer County became a nonentity. In 1906 it reappeared as part of the state of Oklahoma.

Placement of the one hundredth meridian finally became accepted by all concerned parties in 1930, when Oklahoma agreed to its western boundary.

Municipalities into Counties

Strange as it seems, the Constitution of 1836 did not speak directly to the transformation of municipalities into counties. The constitution referred to the municipalities as precincts and made them electoral districts for the First Congress. Those clauses that referred to the election of national lawmakers were the only ones in which local governments were mentioned by name. Thus, Congress implied that they were to be counties, and, in all later legislation, they were referred to as such.

Establishing the physical boundaries of these twenty-three new counties was a demanding task that faced the first Texas Congress, however. The twelve municipalities created by the Mexican government had some boundary descriptions, no matter how vague by today's standards. The following example taken from the Mexican Congressional records for the Municipality of Brazoria gives some idea of the imprecision characteristic of the best descriptions:

Article 1: In the southern portion of the Municipality of Austin a new Municipality shall be formed of which the town of Brazoria shall be the capital.

Article 2: The limits of said Municipality shall be as follows: commencing at the mouth of Clear Creek on Galveston Bay, following the principal branch of said creek to its source, then southwesterly in a straight line to strike the Brazos four leagues above the mouth of Big Creek, thence in a straight line to the confluence of Guajaro Creek and the River St. Bernard.[5]

At its best, the General Council of 1835–36 had not been this specific in its unorthodox creation of municipalities. Similarly, the Constitution of 1836 said nothing about the geography of existing counties other than that they must be surveyed. Consequently, the republic spent inordinate time and effort grappling with problems concerning county boundaries. This difficulty persists today, as neighboring counties duel with each other over adjacent lands.

No accurate map existed in 1836, depicting the Republic of Texas immediately after it gained independence. County boundaries were vaguely known, and surveys were merely a topic of conversation. Maps are available in shops which purport to show the early Republic of Texas, but, by and large, they are inconsistent with each other and based upon questionable data sources.

Map 4-3 (1836) is based on data taken from several sources. The most helpful was Gammel's documentation[6] of the acts of the Mexican Congress and of the General Council as they created municipalities. Other sources include old maps on file in the Texas State Archives in Austin, data obtained from the Texas General Land Office in Austin, and the work of Seymour V. Conner.[7] Numerous other old maps were also consulted for these and other counties.

Of necessity, some boundaries in map 4-3 were arrived at by inference. All had to be consistent with maps of counties that were created in later years and never altered after their creation.

Map 4-4 is an overlay of the original counties on the state map of today; today's counties are designated by dashed lines.

The Texas Constitution did say that the republic would be divided into counties as needed, and it provided that all the laws then in force and not inconsistent with the state constitution would remain in force.

A new county could be created by the Texas Congress, but only upon petition of one hundred free males. The new county had to encompass a minimum of nine hundred square miles.

Each county was assigned a specific number of representatives, and coun-

The Original 23 Counties in 1836.

MAP 4-3. The first twenty-three counties of the Republic of Texas. They had been municipalities under Mexican rule. Map by Luke Gournay.

ties were grouped into senatorial districts. However, the constitution set a
limit on the total number of representatives—forty. The original counties
immediately used thirty-two of this number, leaving only eight for any new
counties.

This restriction soon became a source of anguish and embarrassment for
the Texas Congress. As population grew and new counties were formed, the
eight available congressional seats soon vanished. The Texas Congress tried
to circumvent this dilemma by creating "judicial counties" that had the
customary county offices but were not allowed to participate directly in
congressional elections. Residents of these "judicial counties" would have to
vote in the parent county and would be represented by that county's legislator. Some fifteen counties came about in this way and belong to a group

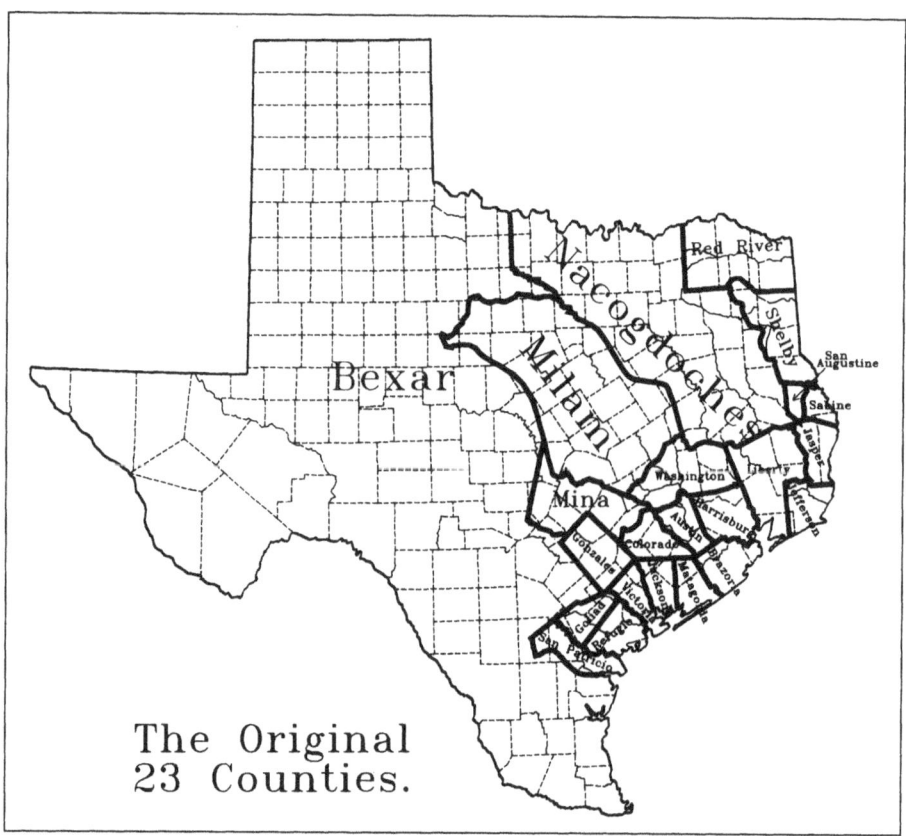

MAP 4-4. The first twenty-three counties (solid lines) are overlaid on the present two hundred fifty-four counties (dashed lines). Map by Luke Gournay.

often called "the phantom counties." This ploy worked until the Texas Supreme Court in 1842 declared that judicial counties were unconstitutional and ordered them dissolved.

The new state constitution, written when Texas joined the United States in 1845, resolved the representation problem. It also added restraints on the formation of new counties. No existing county could be reduced to less than nine hundred square miles by the formation of a new county without the consent of a two-thirds majority of the legislature. The legislature could continue to create new counties, regardless of the sentiments of county residents.

The rules for county creation went unchanged until 1876, when a new state constitution dictated that no new counties of less than nine hundred square miles could be formed out of unorganized land, and that these had to be as square as possible. Counties formed from those already organized had to be at least seven hundred square miles in size, and no parent county could be reduced to less than this minimum. If a county was to be between seven hundred and nine hundred square miles, a two-thirds legislative majority was required. The boundary of a new county had to be at least twelve miles from the seat of the parent county.

Generally, the legislature required that a county seat be located within three to five miles of the county's center. This requirement often dictated the removal of a county seat to another location when a county was subdivided. There is no record to verify the folk belief that the courthouse was not allowed to be no more than a day's horseback ride from any point within the county.

Occasionally new areas became sufficiently populated to have judicial needs but still had too few people to support a county government. In these cases it was common for the legislature to create an "unorganized" county and attach it to a nearby organized county for judicial and tax purposes. Thus we see that some counties came into being years before they were fully organized with a local government.

A legislative act of 1874 specified how an unorganized county could change to organized status. Its citizens had to present a petition with names of 150 qualified voters to the court of the organized county to which the unorganized county was attached. Upon approval, organization could proceed. This rule was amended in 1918 to reduce the number on the petition to 75 voters.

The name of a new county was often proposed in the petition asking for its formation. In some cases, the government, whether the republic or the state, imposed a name in its creating act. The source of some names is unclear. Out of these methods came a list of colorful names that can be divided into several categories.

Forty-two of the two hundred fifty-four Texas counties bear Indian, French, or Spanish names. Ten commemorate such colonizers as Stephen F. Austin, McMullen, and DeWitt. Twelve honor American patriots such as Washington.

Ninety-six counties were named for men who died in the Texas War for Independence, signed the Declaration of Independence from Mexico, or served as statesmen in the Republic of Texas.

Twenty-three have the names of frontiersmen and pioneers.

Eleven honor American statesmen who worked for the annexation of Texas. Ten were named after leaders in Texas since statehood, including jurists, ministers, educators, historians, and statesmen. Thirty-six were named for individuals prominent in the Confederacy during the Civil War.

Rockwall and eight others have geographical names. San Jacinto and Val Verde were named for battles, Live Oak and Orange for trees, and Mason for a fort.

The next chapter traces the rise of new counties and gives a picture of the dynamism of Texas through the years.

Notes

1. H. P. N. Gammel, comp., *The Laws of Texas, 1822–1897*, vol. 1 (Austin, Tex.: Gammel, 1898) page 748.
2. Joseph Milton Nance, *After San Jacinto* (Austin: University of Texas Press, 1932).
3. George Durham, *Taming the Nueces Strip* (Austin: University of Texas Press, 1962).
4. A. W. Neville, *The History of Lamar County* (Paris, Tex.: North Texas Publishing Co., 1926).
5. Gammel, *Laws of Texas*, 1:307.
6. Ibid., vol. 1.
7. Conner, "County Government," 163–200.

5 · Evolution of the Counties

The areas and shapes of the original twenty-three counties changed considerably after 1836. Divisions allowed for the formation of two hundred thirty-one new government entities. Boundaries shifted and warped. In the process, the once immense counties were reduced to reasonable sizes. Map 5-1 illustrates the magnitude of these reductions. The remnants of the original twenty-three are drawn in bold outline over the map of modern Texas.

In this chapter, we follow changes in the Texas map through time. For each year in which counties were created, we show a new map, representing Texas at the end of that year. Bold lines are used to designate the counties created in that year. In some years, the Congress of the Republic or the Texas Legislature created only one new county. In other years, such as 1876, as many as fifty-four new ones appeared. And in some years, no new counties were created.

Boundaries of previously formed counties were adjusted on numerous occasions. Such changes are noted in the text.

The search for accuracy can be endless but must cease at some reasonable point. This philosophy governed the development of these maps. We hope that they represent a best possible compilation of available data, but they are not meant to be taken as a final legal authority.

This chapter is divided into sections, each devoted to a year in which counties were added or abolished. One map is presented in each section, accompanied by a short narrative for each county.

1837 Additions: Map 5-2

FANNIN COUNTY

Created: December 14, 1837, from the recently enlarged Red River County.
Organized: 1840. Lexington was selected as the first county seat, but Old

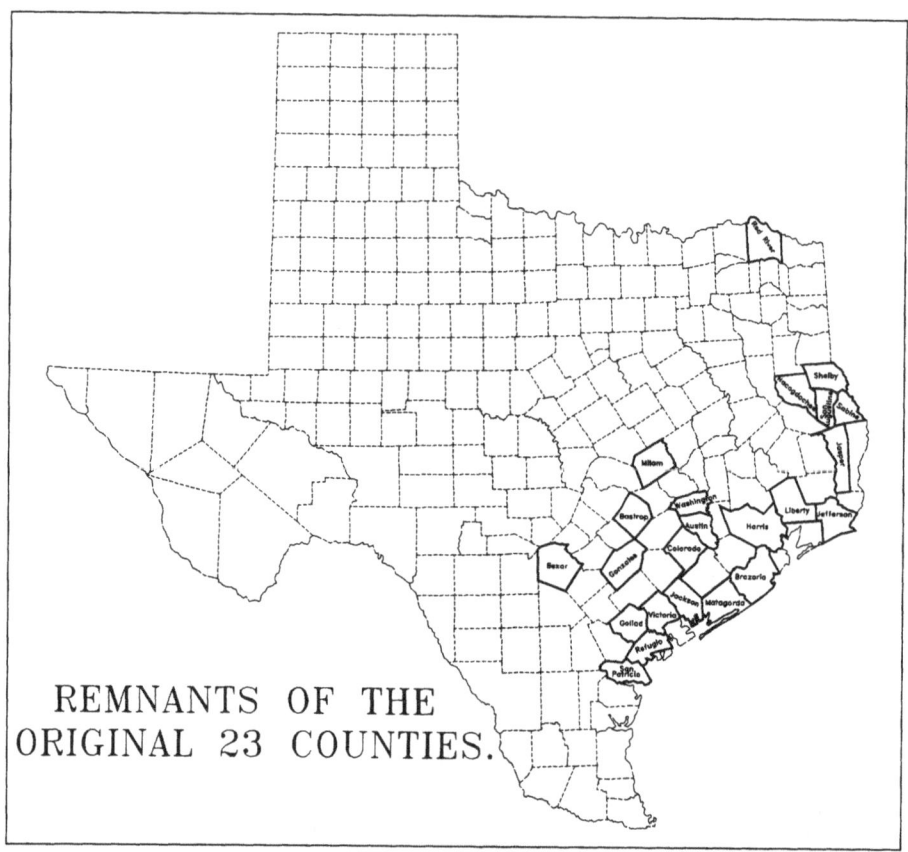

Warren replaced Lexington in 1840. Bois d'Arc changed its name to Bonham and became the county seat on January 16, 1843.

Boundaries: The boundaries described by the Congress of the Republic in 1837 reasonably defined the east and north lines, but the southern and western edges of the original county were open to conjecture. In 1839, the Congress expanded the county and better specified its boundaries.

Named: The county was named for James Walker Fannin. A Georgian born in 1805, he was a cadet at West Point Military Academy. He came to Texas in 1834 and engaged in farming for a while before serving in the war against Mexico. While leading four hundred troops, he was overtaken by Mexican cavalry about two miles from Coleto. Wounded in this fight, Fannin surrendered himself and his troops. (Accounts of what followed are contradictory, but most agree that there was a surrender.) He and his troops were captured

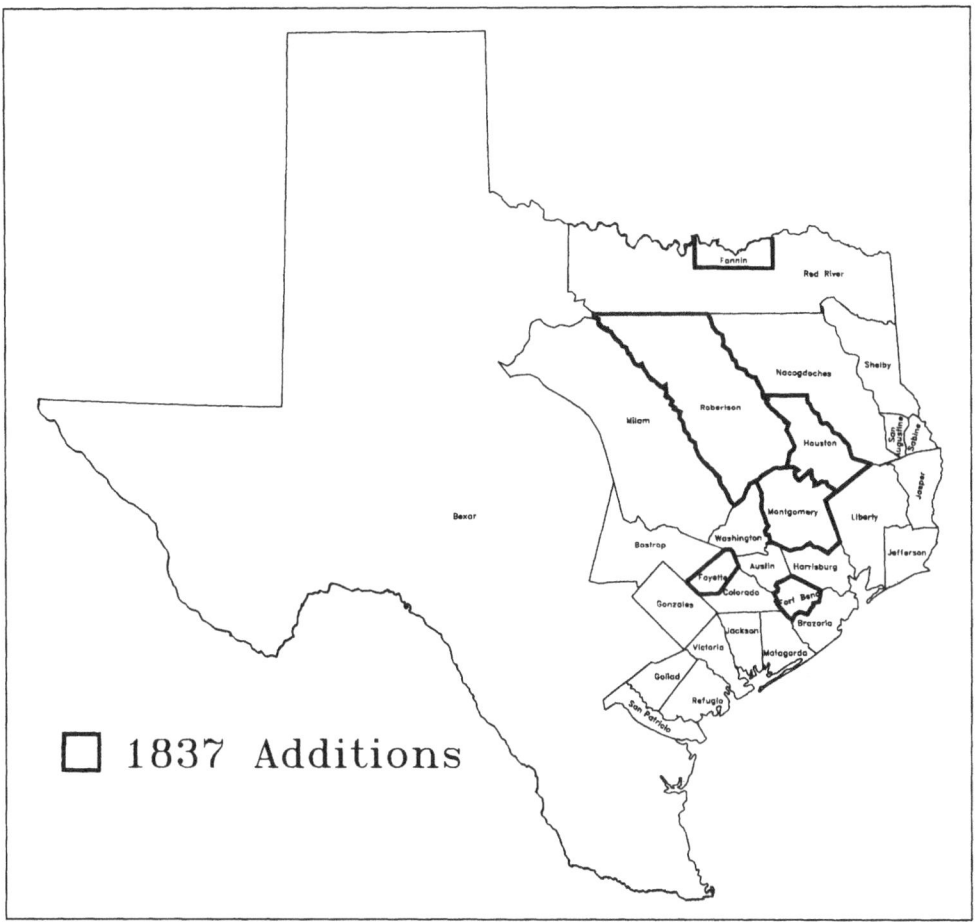

MAP 5-2. Changes in Texas counties, 1837. Map by Luke Gournay.

and marched back to Goliad, where all were shot by the Mexican army on March 27, 1836.

FAYETTE COUNTY

Created: Out of Bastrop County on December 14, 1837. This county, which originally formed part of the Stephen F. Austin Colony, was settled by members of the "Old Three Hundred."

Organized: January 1838. LaGrange, named for the French home of General de Lafayette, became the undisputed county seat.

Boundaries: Parts of Fayette County later were taken to form Lavaca and Lee counties. The southwestern boundary was adjusted on May 3, 1838.

Named: For the Marquis de Lafayette, a captain of Dragoons in the French army. Inspired by the cause of American independence, he attempted, unsuccessfully, to move France to aid the colonists. In frustration, he purchased a ship of his own and set sail for North America with a group of friends. He and his ship were captured en route and sent to Spain. He managed to escape and soon was on the high seas again. Lafayette landed at Georgetown, South Carolina, and joined in the fray. He fought with General Washington and was wounded at the Battle of Brandywine. He returned to France but revisited America several times.

FORT BEND COUNTY

Created: From Austin County on December 29, 1837.
Organized: January 1838, with Richmond named as the county seat.
Boundaries: The line between Fort Bend and Austin counties was modified on February 4, 1841, and again on March 24, 1846.
Named: For an old fort built in a bend of the Brazos River in 1818.

HOUSTON COUNTY

Created: June 8, 1837, from Nacogdoches County.
Organized: 1837, with Crockett, located near the busy Old San Antonio Road, as the county seat.
Boundaries: In the years following its creation, pieces of Houston County were used to create Trinity, Anderson, and part of Henderson counties.
Named: For Sam Houston, the central figure in the history of the Republic of Texas. Houston came from Virginia via Tennessee and had spent time with the Cherokee Indians. In Texas, he headed the fight for independence from Mexico and became the first president of the new republic, then congressman, president again, United States senator, and governor of the State of Texas.

MONTGOMERY COUNTY

Created: December 14, 1837, from Washington County.
Organized: In 1837, with the county seat at the old town of Montgomery. Subsequently, the county seat bounced to Willis in 1874 and back to Montgomery in 1880. Then, in 1889, the new town of Conroe established its claim as the county seat, and such it has remained.
Boundaries: Modified in 1838 and in 1840.
Named: For Richard Montgomery, an Irishman, who settled in New York in 1773. He was appointed a brigadier general in the American Revolution in 1775, fought against the British, and was killed in Quebec on November 31, 1775.

ROBERTSON COUNTY

Created: December 14, 1837, from Milam County. The creating act placed the northern boundary of the county at "the northern edge of the Cross

Timbers," although no one has ever known just where this line was meant to be. County boundaries were further defined in 1846.

Organized: In 1838, with Old Franklin as county seat. In 1850, Wheelock became the base of government, and Old Franklin turned into a ghost town. An 1854 election to move the county seat failed in its objective, but in 1855 Owensville was accepted by a majority of voters. In 1870, Calvert took over as county seat, and Owensville in its turn became a ghost town. In 1879, the coming of the International–Great Northern Railroad enabled the new town of Morgan to become the county seat. Morgan was renamed Franklin, in honor of the original Old Franklin.

Named: For Sterling Clack Robertson, a Tennessean who fought the Indians and the British in the War of 1812. After coming to Texas in 1823, Robertson managed a colony, played a role in the Convention of 1836, and signed the Texas Declaration of Independence. Heading an infantry company, he marched to Harrisburg but did not find Sam Houston in time to be at San Jacinto. He was elected senator for the First Congress of the Republic of Texas and then turned his attention to his business, which he had neglected.

1838 Addition: Map 5-3

GALVESTON COUNTY

Created: May 15, 1838, out of Brazoria County, one of the original twenty-three counties.

Organized: 1839, with the town of Galveston as county seat.

Boundaries: No divisions were made in Galveston County after 1838, except for minor changes to include or exclude some islands off the mainland.

Named: For the Spanish name *Galvez*, shared by José de Galvez, Matías de Galvez, and Bernardo de Galvez. All three were connected with the government of Spain and the province of Mexico, serving as assistants or viceroys of the region. Perhaps the most dashing was Bernardo de Galvez, who served as captain-general of Havana, Louisiana, and Florida. He came to Mexico accompanied by his beautiful young French wife, Felicitas St. Maxent, a native of New Orleans. His inauguration in Mexico was brilliant, as was his entire career.

1839 Addition: Map 5-4

HARRISON COUNTY

Created: January 28, 1839, out of Shelby County.

Organized: Marshall became the county seat when the county was organized on June 18, 1842.

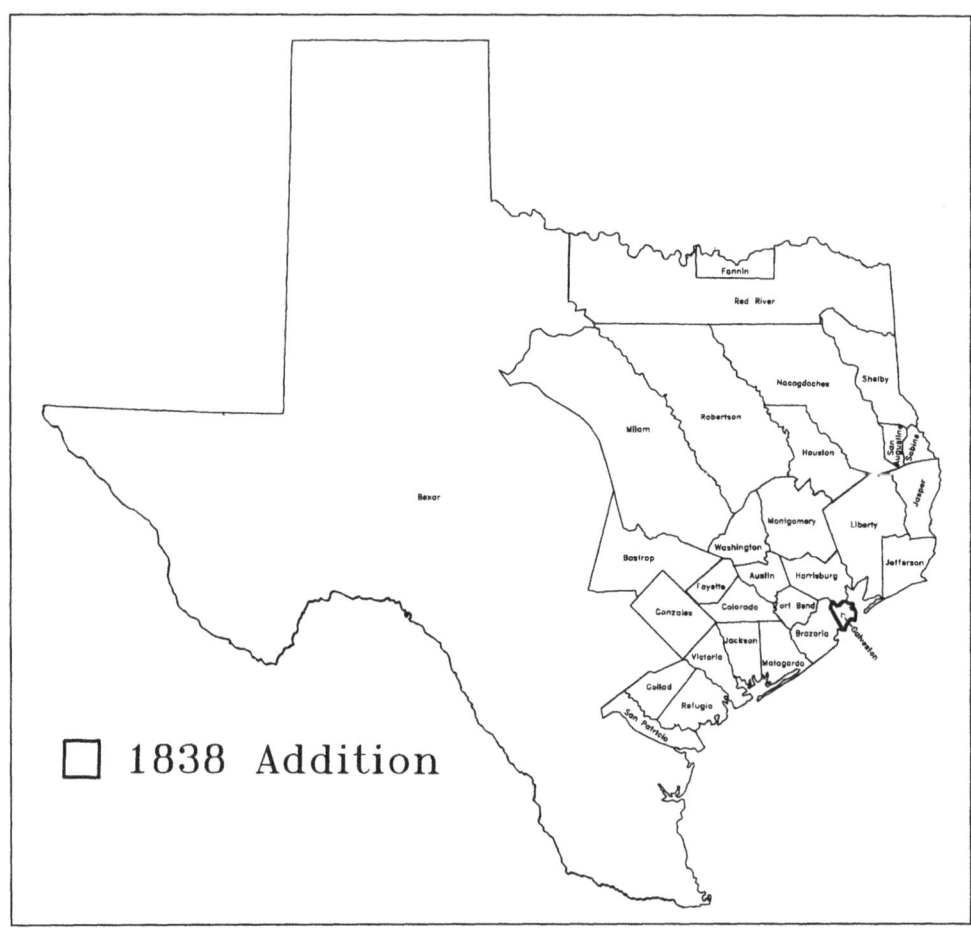

MAP 5-3. Changes in Texas counties, 1838. Map by Luke Gournay.

Boundaries: A portion of Harrison County was assigned to Bowie County on January 8, 1844.

Named: For Jonas Harrison, who came from New Jersey with his wife and children in 1821. In the 1832 and 1833 conventions with the Mexican government, in which separate statehood was requested, Harrison represented his area, then known as Tenaha.

1840 Additions: Map 5-5

TRAVIS COUNTY

Created: January 25, 1840, from Bastrop County, one of the original twenty-three. Travis County initially contained forty thousand square miles.

Organized: Organization took place on April 8, 1843, with Austin named

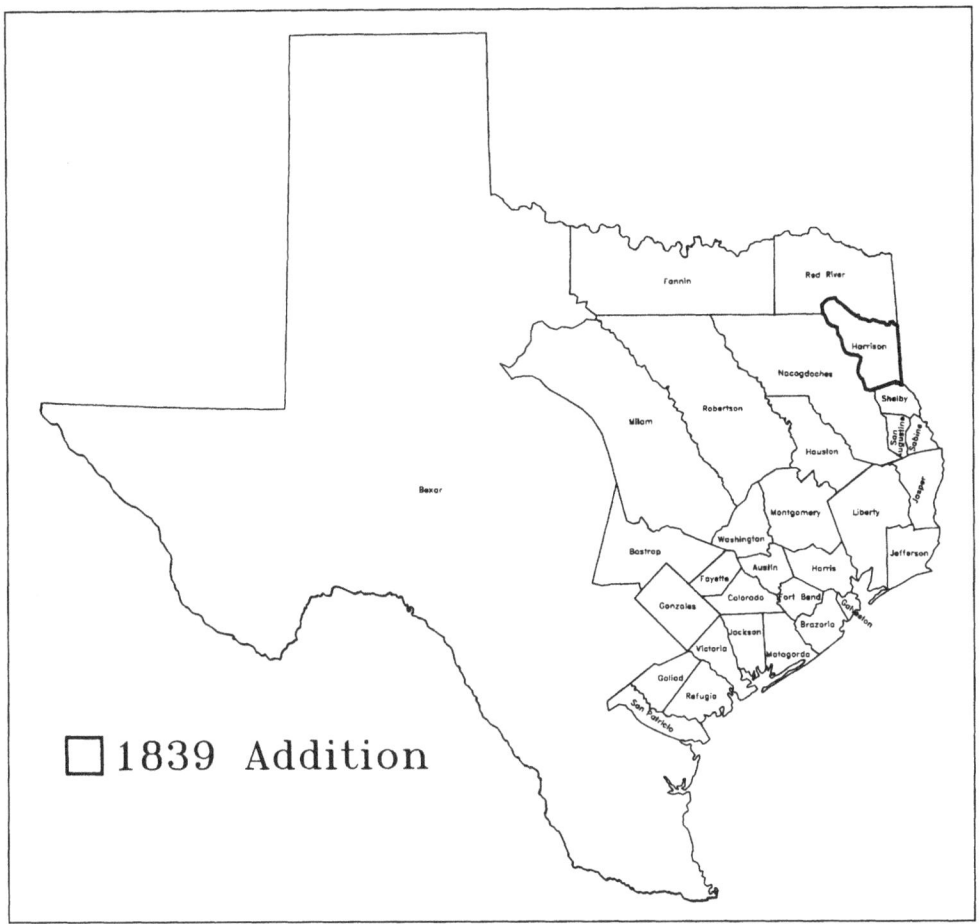

MAP 5-4. Changes in Texas counties, 1839. Map by Luke Gournay.

as county seat. Stephen F. Austin had chosen this area for one of his colonies.

Boundaries: The subsequent creation of numerous counties from Travis reduced its area to the present 1,022 square miles.

Named: For one of the best-known Texas heroes, William Barret Travis. The county seat was named for Stephen Fuller Austin. Travis arrived in Anahuac in 1831, having left his wife, two children, and an established law practice behind in Alabama to join the campaign for Texas independence. He served in that struggle from Gonzales to the Alamo. As commander of the Alamo, Travis gave his life, fighting to the death.

BOWIE COUNTY

Created: December 17, 1840, out of Red River County.

Organized: 1846, with Boston as county seat. A later survey showed that

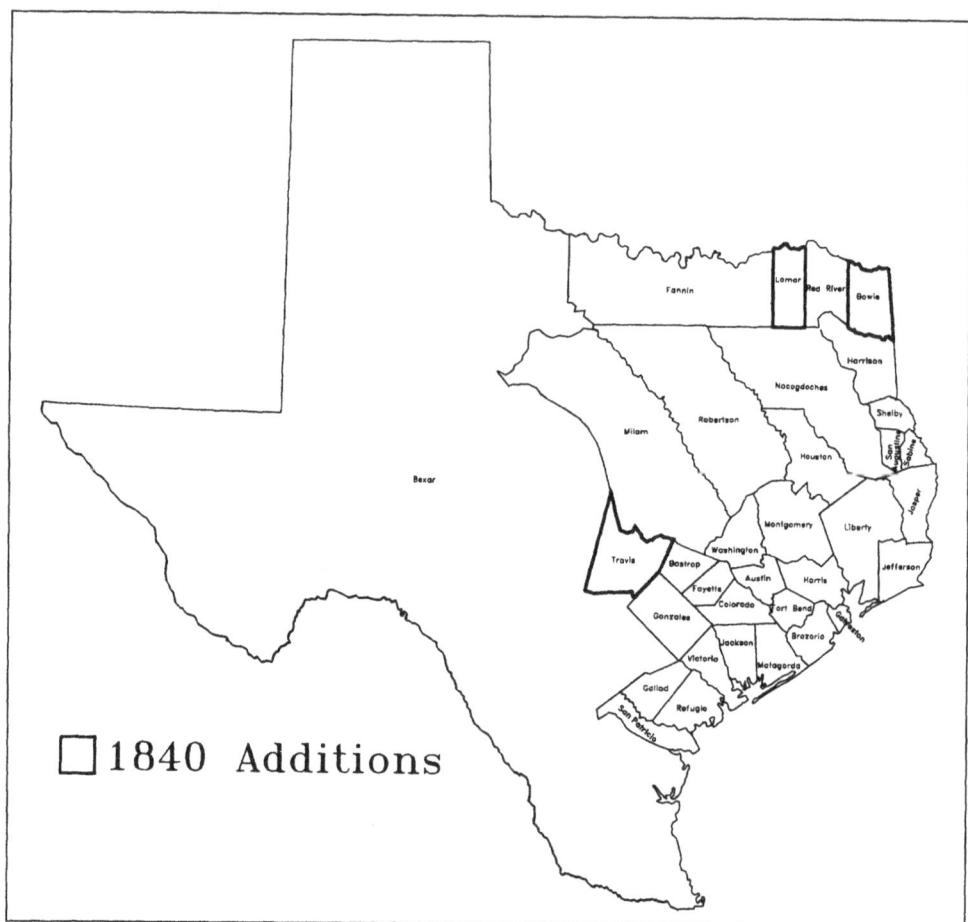

MAP 5-5. Changes in Texas counties, 1840. Map by Luke Gournay.

Boston was about five miles from the center of the county, so the court-house was moved north to the present site of Boston. The old settlement to the south is now called Old Boston.

Named: For James Bowie, a patriot of the Alamo. Raised in Louisiana, he became active in the Texas Revolution in 1835. After taking part in the capture of Bexar, Bowie met his end at the Alamo.

LAMAR COUNTY

Created: December 17, 1840—on the same day and by the same congressio-nal act as Bowie. Both counties were formed out of Red River County.

Organized: In February 1841. The first county seat was located in the village of Lafayette, about eight miles northwest of what is now Paris. Two years later the seat of government was moved to the settlement of Mount

Vernon, where court was held in a tavern. Soon thereafter, the people voted to relocate the county seat to the town of Paris (originally Pinhook), where George Wright had donated fifty acres for this purpose.

Boundaries: The southern half of Lamar County was taken to make Hopkins County in 1846. In 1870, Delta County was shaped from parts of Lamar and Hopkins. The northeastern corner of Hopkins County was added to Lamar County on November 17, 1871.

Named: for Mirabeau Buonaparte Lamar. A native of Georgia, he came to Texas in 1835, in time to join the Battle of San Jacinto. He was elected vice-president of the Republic of Texas under Sam Houston, then elected second president of the republic. Lamar later served as Texas' minister to Argentina.

1841 Addition: Map 5-6

BRAZOS COUNTY

Created: January 30, 1841, out of Robertson and Washington counties. Originally named Navasota County, in 1842 the county was renamed Brazos.

Organized: February 6, 1843. Boonville was chosen as county seat. In 1866, the Houston and Texas Central Railroad came through this area, and the town of Bryan, three miles west of Boonville, became the county seat. In 1876, the Agricultural and Mechanical College of Texas was established at Bryan, securing the town's place as the county seat.

Boundaries: Present Brazos County originally formed part of Stephen F. Austin's second colony. The area was included in part of the Municipality of Washington under the Mexican government. In 1841, the judicial counties of Burnet, Menard, Neches, Panola, Paschal, Spring Creek, and Ward were created by the Congress of the Republic. The next year the Texas Supreme Court declared all of them unconstitutional and abolished them. Some reappeared under the same names in following years: Panola in 1846, Burnet in 1852, Menard in 1858, and Ward in 1887.

Named: For the river, the word in Spanish means *arms* (of the body).

1843 Addition: Map 5-7

RUSK COUNTY

Created: January 16, 1843, from Nacogdoches County.

Organized: February 6, 1843. Centrally located, Henderson was chosen as county seat.

Boundaries: The Congress of the Republic modified the eastern boundary in December 1844 and again in 1845.

Named: For Thomas Jefferson Rusk, a South Carolinian who, in 1834,

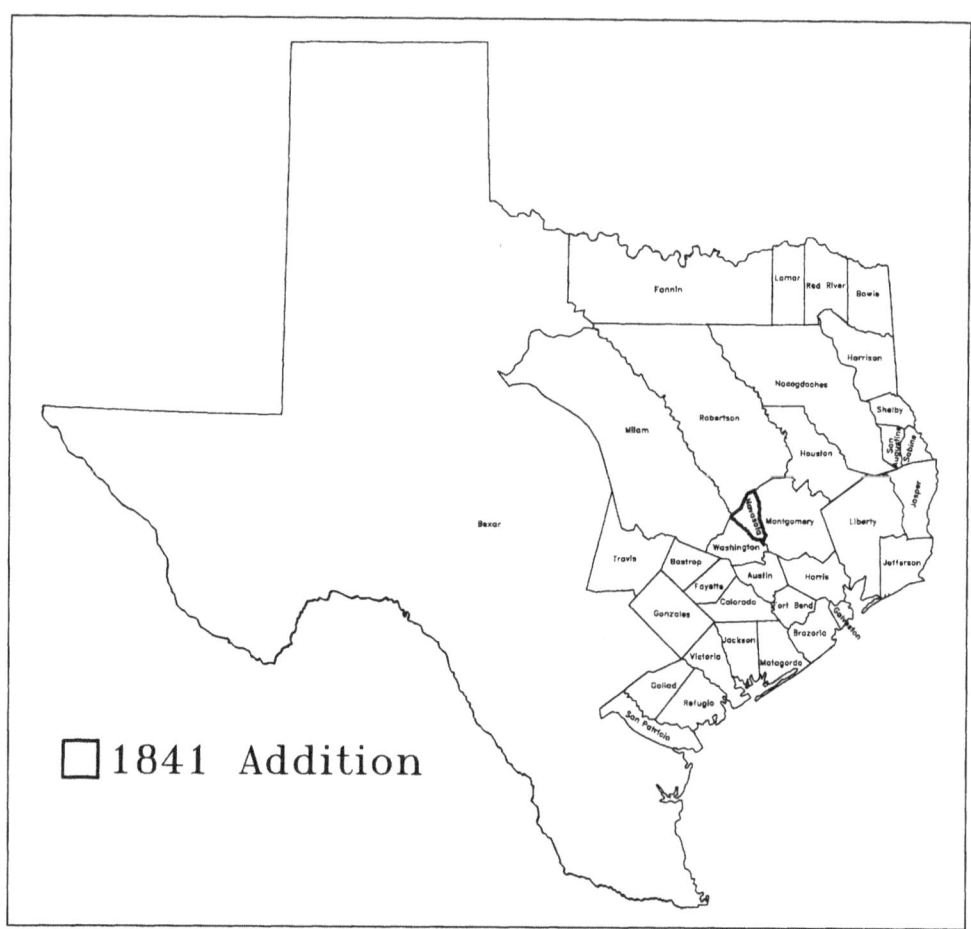

MAP 5-6. Changes in Texas counties, 1841. Map by Luke Gournay.

chased some swindlers into Texas. Rusk stayed, settling in Nacogdoches at the outbreak of the Texas Revolution. He signed the Declaration of Independence and was at the Battle of San Jacinto. Rusk held many important positions in the new republic's government, including secretary of war, congressman, and chief justice of the supreme court. He died by his own hand on July 29, 1857, and is buried in Nacogdoches.

1846 Additions: Map 5-8

The first legislature of the new State of Texas met in 1846. One of its first acts was to originate thirty-one new counties. A brief overview of these governmental entities follows.

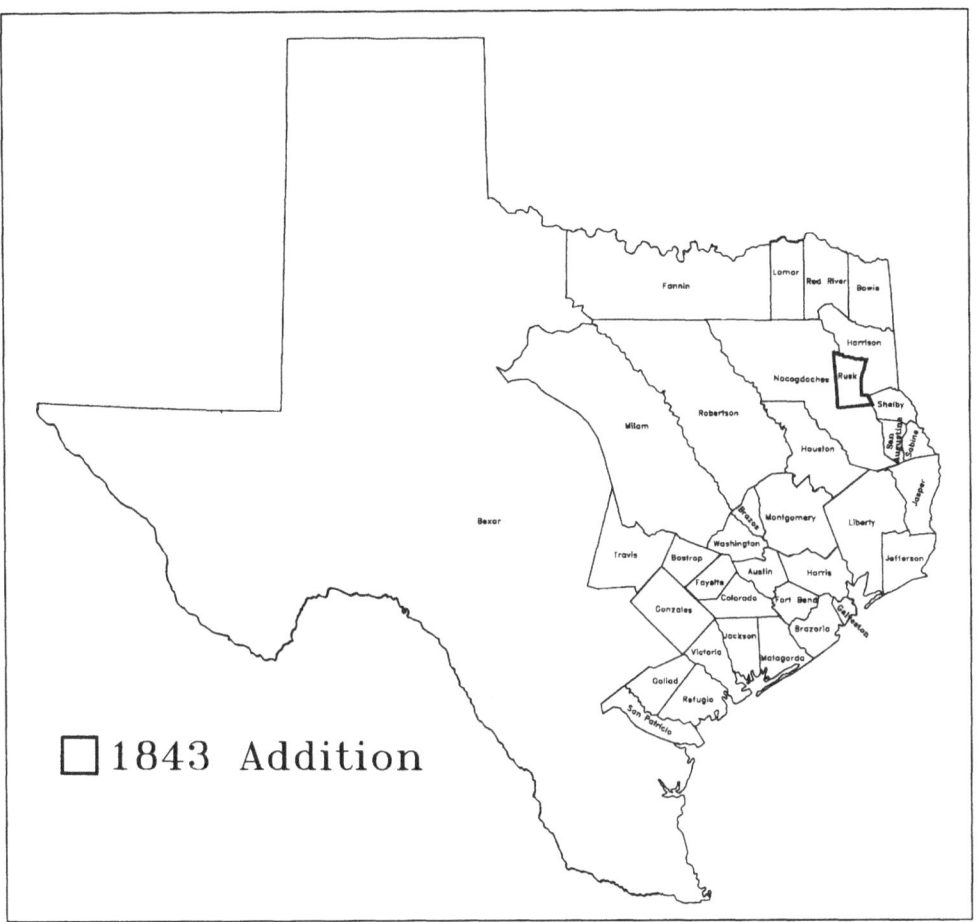

□ 1843 Addition

MAP 5-7. Changes in Texas counties, 1843. Map by Luke Gournay.

ANDERSON COUNTY

Created: March 24, 1846, from Houston County, one of the original twenty-three counties.

Organized: July 13, 1846. Old Fort Houston served as the county seat and was the first Texas town to bear Sam Houston's name. A year later, Fort Houston was found to be two miles off the center of the county. A central site was chosen and named Palestine after the town of Palestine, Illinois. This was the former home of Daniel Parker who was a delegate to the 1835 Consultation from Nacadoches and who opened the 1836 convention with a prayer.

Named: For Kenneth Lewis Anderson, vice-president of the Republic of Texas from 1844 until its annexation.

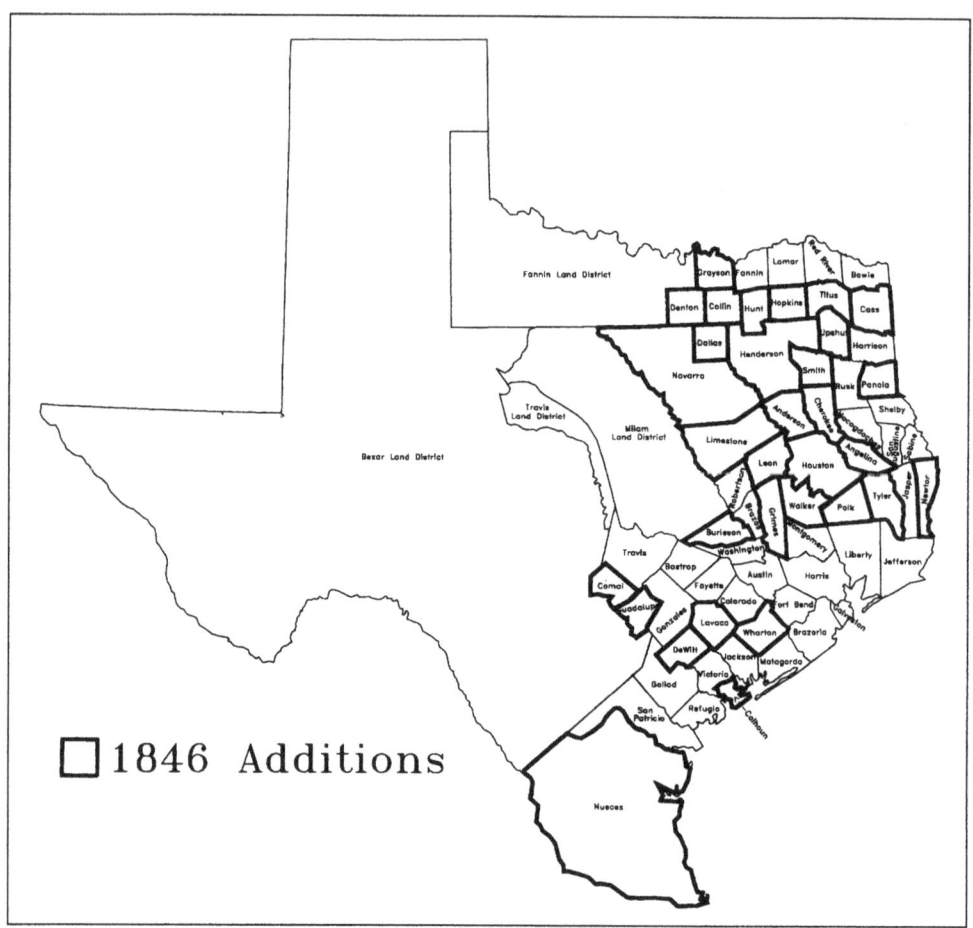

MAP 5-8. Changes in Texas counties, 1846. Map by Luke Gournay.

ANGELINA COUNTY

Created: April 22, 1846, out of Nacogdoches County. Under Mexican rule, this region was part of the Municipality of Nacogdoches.

Organized: July 13, 1846, with Marion named as county seat. Originally called McNeill's Landing, Marion lost the contest for government seat to Jonesville in 1854 and became extinct at the turn of the century. Jonesville, now a ghost town, was replaced by Homer on February 3, 1858. In 1885, the Kansas City and Gulf Short Line Railway Company built a new townsite and named it Lufkin. Because of the railroad traffic, the town grew rapidly; not long afterward, in 1892, this town became county seat.

Named: For the stream whose name means "Little Angel" in Spanish.

Created: March 24, 1846, out of Milam and Washington counties. The county was divided by the old San Antonio Road; that part of the county south of the road had been in Stephen F. Austin's first colony and that part north of the road in Robertson's colony.

Organized: July 13, 1846, with Caldwell named as the county seat.

Boundaries: Burleson County underwent minor boundary changes in 1846 and 1870, with the line between it and Brazos County shifted.

Named: For Gen. Edward Burleson, who was a colonel at the Battle of San Jacinto. He also was brigadier general of the Texas militia in 1837 and colonel in the Texas army in 1838. Elected vice president of the Republic of Texas in 1841, Burleson ran for president in 1843 but was defeated by Anson Jones. After statehood, he was elected to the Texas Senate and became president of that body.

Created: Out of Jackson, Matagorda, and Victoria counties, on March 24, 1846.

Organized: July 13, 1846, with the town of Lavaca serving as the first county seat. In the 1850s, when the Indianola Railroad was built into the area, the county seat was moved into Indianola, formerly Powder Horn. A hurricane destroyed the town of Indianola in 1886, and it never was rebuilt. At that time, Lavaca (by then called Port Lavaca) again became the county seat.

Boundaries: A boundary change occurred on February 11, 1860.

Named: For John C. Calhoun, noted United States congressman and senator, secretary of state under President Monroe, and vice president of the United States. Calhoun supported the annexation of Texas and prepared a treaty of annexation.

Created: April 25, 1846, out of Bowie County.

Organized: July 13, 1846, with Jefferson chosen as the county seat. The first court was held at the tavern house of William Perry. In 1860, when Marion County was created, Jefferson became its county seat and Linden was named the seat of Cass County. The latter county underwent a name change in 1861, when the legislature chose to call it Davis in honor of Jefferson Davis. In 1871, the name was changed back to Cass.

Named: For George Lewis Cass, a United States senator from Michigan who encouraged the annexation of Texas.

CHEROKEE COUNTY

Created: Out of the original Nacogdoches County on April 11, 1846.
Organized: July 13, 1846. The town of Rusk was made the county seat.
Named: For the Cherokee Indians with whom Sam Houston lived for several years.

COLLIN COUNTY

Created: April 3, 1846, out of Fannin County.
Organized: July 13, 1846, when Buckner became the county seat. The legislative act creating the county specified that the county seat must be within three miles of the county's center, and surveys revealed that Buckner was "out of bounds." In 1848, when another election was called, McKinney, more centrally located, was chosen as the county seat.
Boundaries: The county was located in what was then Peters' Colony, with its headquarters located about five miles southwest of present McKinney. Preston Road was used by immigrants into the area.
Named: Collin McKinney, one of the early settlers, who was born in New Jersey in 1776. After coming to Texas in 1824, he was elected a member of the Constitutional Convention in 1836. McKinney was a signer of the Texas Declaration of Independence.

COMAL COUNTY

Created: March 24, 1846, out of Travis and Bexar counties.
Organized: March 24, 1846. New Braunfels was named the county seat.
Boundaries: The county line was modified on February 8, 1871.
Named: For a stream crossed by Spanish explorers. The name also comes from a Spanish word meaning a flat pan used for cooking.

DALLAS COUNTY

Created: March 30, 1846, out of parts of Robertson and Nacogdoches counties.
Organized: July 10, 1846. The town of Dallas was named temporary county seat. A contest for county seat arose among Dallas, Hord's Ridge, and Cedar Springs. Dallas won. The area of Dallas County was originally in Peters' Colony.
Named: Probably named for George Miflin Dallas, a Philadelphian born in 1792. The son of the secretary of state of the United States, George Dallas took a law degree at Princeton College. He served in the United States Senate in 1831, before being appointed minister to Russia. Although there is no evidence that George Miflin Dallas ever traveled to Texas, his name was chosen because of his strong voice in favor of annexation.

DENTON COUNTY

Created: Out of Fannin County on April 11, 1846.
Organized: July 13, 1846, with Pinckneyville selected as the first county seat—because of its location away from the center of the county, a poor choice. The second Texas Legislature authorized moving the county seat four miles north to Alton, another town unsuitable because of the lack of good water. On November 26, 1850, the third Texas Legislature moved the county seat, along with the name of Alton, to Alexander Cannon's homestead on Hickory Creek, five miles south of the present town of Denton. In an election on April 22, 1857, voters chose to move the town and change its name from Alton to Denton.
Named: For John B. Denton, born in Tennessee, who became a famous preacher and orator. He settled in Red River County, where he also practiced law. Denton was ambushed and killed by Indians in 1841.

DEWITT COUNTY

Created: March 24, 1846, from Gonzales, Goliad, and Victoria counties.
Organized: July 13, 1846, when a courthouse was built at Cameron. In the next four years, the county seat was moved four times. Each move was dictated by an election, and most of the elections were conducted amid such turmoil that either an appeal, a recount, or a Supreme Court ruling ensued. On November 28, 1850, the county seat went to Clinton, near Chisholm's ferry. Clinton remained the center of county government until Cuero became county seat in 1876.
Named: For Graham C. DeWitt, a Kentuckian who established a successful colony in the area. His colony covered what is presently Caldwell, DeWitt, Gonzales, and Guadalupe counties, as well as parts of Comal, Fayette, Lavaca, and Victoria counties.

GRAYSON COUNTY

Created: March 17, 1846, out of the large Fannin Land District.
Organized: July 13, 1846, with Sherman as the county seat.
Boundaries: A minor boundary change occurred in 1848. In 1856, the western boundary with Cooke County was adjusted.
Named: For another Kentuckian, Peter W. Grayson, who came to Texas in 1832. In 1835, he joined in the fight against Mexico. Afterward, he served in the Provisional Government before becoming state attorney general.

GRIMES COUNTY

Created: April 6, 1846, out of Montgomery County. Grimes was originally a part of the Municipality of Viesca.
Organized: July 15, 1846. The county seat was placed at Fanthorp's Inn,

Evolution of Counties • 49

later renamed Anderson. A petition to transfer the county seat to Navasota led to an unsuccessful election in 1871.

Named: For Jesse Grimes, a North Carolinian who came to Texas in 1829 to farm. He was chosen as a member of the Convention of 1833, was a member of the Consultation and of the Convention of 1836, and was a signer of the Texas Declaration of Independence. One of his sons, Charles Grimes, was killed at the Alamo at the age of eighteen.

GUADALUPE COUNTY

Created: March 30, 1846, from Bexar County.
Organized: July 13, 1846, when Seguin was chosen as county seat.
Named: For the Guadalupe River, first called "Our Lady of Guadalupe" by Alonso de Leon in 1689. This name was applied to the county in 1842, when the Congress of the Republic made it a judicial district, and again in 1846 when it became a legitimate county.

HENDERSON COUNTY

Created: April 27, 1846, from Nacogdoches and Houston counties.
Organized: July 13, 1846, when Athens was chosen as the county seat.
Boundaries: Small boundary changes were made in 1848 and 1850.
Named: For James Pinckney Henderson, the first governor of the State of Texas. Originally from North Carolina, he became a Texan and served as Texas' minister to England and France, where he negotiated treaties of commerce and navigation with these countries. In 1844, he served as Texas' special minister to the United States. In 1845, he was elected the first governor of the new state.

HOPKINS COUNTY

Created: March 25, 1846, out of Lamar and Nacogdoches counties.
Organized: July 13, 1846, with Tarrant named as county seat. In 1870, parts of Hopkins County were used to form Rains and Delta counties, and part of it was removed to Lamar County in 1871. As a result of these boundary changes, the county seat was moved from Tarrant to Sulphur Springs on July 1, 1870.
Boundaries: A change in boundary between Hopkins and Wood counties occurred in 1874.
Named: For the pioneer Hopkins family who migrated from Indiana in 1840.

HUNT COUNTY

Created: Out of Fannin and Nacogdoches counties on April 11, 1846.
Organized: July 12, 1846, with Greenville as the county seat.

Named: For Gen. Memucan Hunt, who came to Texas from North Carolina by way of Mississippi. Hunt served in various high governmental positions.

Created: April 6, 1846, from Colorado, Jackson, Gonzales, and Victoria counties.
Organized: 1852, after an intense struggle among Hallettsville, Rock Springs, and Petersburg to become county seat. Hallettsville won.
Boundaries: The boundary between Lavaca and Gonzales counties was changed on August 21, 1856, attaching a part of Gonzales County to Lavaca County.
Named: For the Lavaca River. In Spanish, the words *la vaca* mean *the cow*.

LEON COUNTY

Created: From Robertson County on March 17, 1846. This sector was originally part of the Stephen Austin and Samuel Williams colonial grant.
Organized: July 13, 1846, with the town of Leona chosen as county seat. A population shift caused the county seat to be moved to Centerville in 1851.
Named: For Martín de León, a Mexican rancher in Texas who was active in the revolt against Spain. He later had a land grant on the Guadalupe River and established the town of Victoria. Others claim that the county's name was derived from *leon*, a yellow wolf of the region.

LIMESTONE COUNTY

Created: From Robertson County on April 11, 1846.
Organized: With Springfield as the seat of justice, on August 18, 1846. Groesbeck took over as county seat in 1873, after the Houston and Texas Central Railroad bypassed Springfield.
Named: For the prolific limestone outcroppings found in the area.

NAVARRO COUNTY

Created: April 25, 1846, from Robertson County.
Organized: July 13, 1846, with Corsicana named as the county seat.
Named: For José Antonio Navarro, who, as a senator in the First Texas Legislature, was instrumental in the county's organization. The county seat was named after his parents' place of origin, Corsica.

NEWTON COUNTY

Created: From Jasper County on April 22, 1846.
Organized: July 13, 1846, with Newton as the county seat. County government moved to Burkeville in 1848, as the legislature felt that the inhabitants of Newton had not established a seat of justice. Newton resumed its position as county seat in 1853.

Named: Along with Jasper County, this county was named for two young men who were heroes in the American Revolutionary War, John Newton and William Jasper. William was killed in action in 1779; John died of smallpox while a British prisoner in 1780.

NUECES COUNTY

Created: April 11, 1846, from San Patricio County.
Organized: July 12, 1846, with Corpus Christi as county seat.
Boundaries: Minor changes were made in the boundaries between San Patricio and Nueces counties in 1858.
Named: By the Spaniards for the many pecan trees seen along the banks of the river. *Nueces* means *nuts* in Spanish.

PANOLA COUNTY

Created: From parts of Shelby and Harrison counties on March 30, 1846.
Organized: In September 1846, when Pulaski was selected as county seat. Two years later, Carthage replaced Pulaski.
Named: For the Indian word, *ponolo*, meaning cotton.

POLK COUNTY

Created: March 30, 1846, from Liberty County.
Organized: July 10, 1846, with Livingston as the county seat.
Named: For James Knox Polk, who was United States president when Texas was annexed, when the Mexican-American War was fought, and at the time Polk County was formed.

SMITH COUNTY

Created: April 11, 1846, from part of Nacogdoches County.
Organized: July 10, 1846, with Tyler named the county seat.
Named: For Gen. James Smith. A wealthy plantation owner in Nacogdoches County, he left to take part in the Texas Revolution and served in the army during later crises. He was newly elected to the Texas House of Representatives when the bill to create Smith County was passed.

TITUS COUNTY

Created: Out of Bowie and Red River counties on May 11, 1846.
Organized: July 13, 1846, with Mount Pleasant named as county seat.
Named: For Andrew Jackson Titus, a native Tennessean who became a Texan in 1839, just in time to serve in the Mexican War. After the war, as a state legislator, he worked diligently to see that Texas became annexed to the United States.

Created: Out of the original Liberty County on April 3, 1846.
Organized: July 13, 1846, under direction from the legislature to locate the county seat within five miles of the county's center. Town Bluff acted as temporary county seat until Woodville was selected.
Named: For United States President John Tyler.

Created: From Nacogdoches and Harrison counties on April 27, 1846.
Organized: July 13, 1846. Gilmer was selected to be county seat.
Named: For Abel Packer Upshur, who began negotiations for annexation of Texas. At the time, Upshur was secretary of state in President Tyler's cabinet. Gilmer's name honors Thomas W. Gilmer, who served with valor in the United States Navy.

Created: April 6, 1846, from Montgomery County.
Organized: July 18, 1846, with Huntsville named county seat.
Boundaries: Walker County lost acreage to San Jacinto County in 1870.
Named: For Robert John Walker, who, as a United States senator, introduced a resolution acknowledging the independence of the Republic of Texas. Later, he promoted legislation for the annexation of Texas and provided strong support for its passage.

Though Walker was honored throughout Texas, his popularity ended abruptly when he sided with the Union in the Civil War. On December 10, 1863, the Texas Legislature took its revenge for Walker's position. Instead of changing the name of the county, they changed the person for whom it was named. The new honoree was Samuel H. Walker, a Texas Ranger who died in the Mexican-American War.

Created: 1846, from two original counties: Jackson and Matagorda.
Organized: 1846, with the town of Wharton as county seat.
Named: For William H. and John A. Wharton, both lawyers who were elected to various political posts.

1848 Additions: Map 5-9

In 1848, the Texas Legislature added twelve counties to the existing map. Among this dozen was Santa Fe County, which has already been described in chapter 4 (see map 4-2). The other eleven are discussed below.

Evolution of Counties • 53

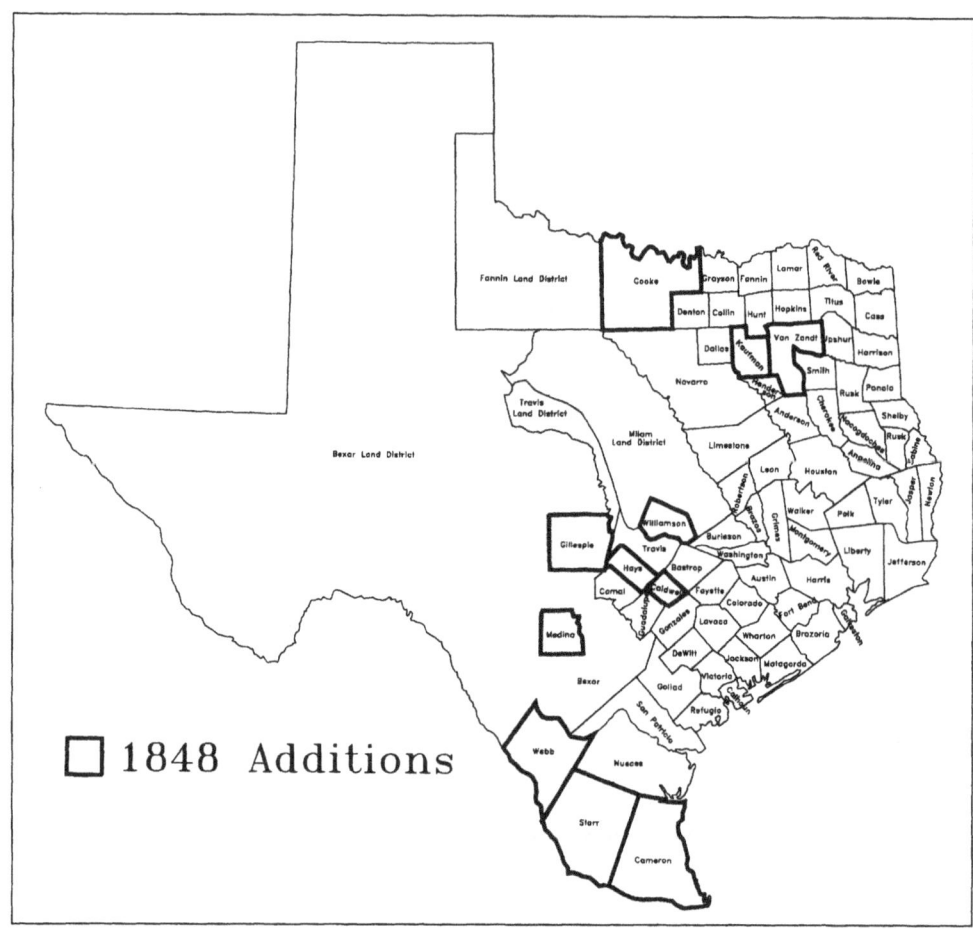

MAP 5-9. Changes in Texas counties, 1848. Map by Luke Gournay.

CALDWELL COUNTY

Created: March 6, 1848, out of Bastrop and Gonzales counties.
Organized: August, 7, 1848. As directed by the legislative act, the commissioners made Lockhart the county seat.
Named: For a Kentuckian, Mathew Caldwell. A signer of the Texas Declaration of Independence, he also represented the Municipality of Sabine at the Convention of 1836. Caldwell served in various positions in the Texas army and took part in the battle against Mexican General Woll in 1842.

CAMERON COUNTY

Created: Out of Nueces County on February 12, 1848.
Organized: August 7, 1848. Santa Rita (or Rita Santa) was the first county seat, but Brownsville won that honor in December 1848.

Boundaries: Redefined in 1851 and again in 1870. In 1871, changes were made to the county lines of Cameron County, as well as Duval, Encinal, Hidalgo, Nueces, Starr, Webb, and Zapata counties.
Named: For Ewen Cameron, a Scotsman who arrived in Texas in 1837, in time to fight in the Battle of Mier. He was taken prisoner and, on Santa Ana's orders, executed in 1843.

COOKE COUNTY

Created: Out of Fannin County on March 20, 1848.
Organized: March 10, 1849, when Gainesville was chosen to be county seat.
Boundaries: The line between Cooke and Grayson counties was redefined in 1856.
Named: For William G. Cooke, a Virginian who moved to New Orleans to do business but responded to a call for volunteers to aid Texas in its fight for independence. He was a captain of the New Orleans Grays who followed Ben Milam into San Antonio. Cooke then served with General Houston at the Battle of San Jacinto. He was unfortunate enough to be assigned to the ill-fated Santa Fe expedition. Cooke was captured and taken to Mexico but released in 1842. He later married Angela Navarro, a niece of José Antonio Navarro.

GILLESPIE COUNTY

Created: February 28, 1848, out of Travis and Bexar counties.
Organized: June 3, 1848, with Fredericksburg as county seat.
Named: For Richard Addison Gillespie, a Kentuckian who came to Texas in 1837. He fought in several battles with Indians and Mexicans. Gillespie died on the battlefield in 1846.

HAYS COUNTY

Created: Out of Travis County on March 1, 1848.
Organized: August 7, 1848. Abiding by the legislative act, commissioners made San Marcos the county seat.
Named: For John Coffee Hayes, a Tennessean, also known as Jack Hayes. Hayes led a group of Texas Rangers who had much to do with bringing peace and tranquillity to the state. He was deeply involved in the Texas Revolution and the Mexican-American War. In 1849, he led a large caravan of "forty-niners" to California, where he was made sheriff of San Francisco. He bought a large Spanish grant on the shore of the bay opposite San Francisco and laid out a city. Hays called it Oakland.

KAUFMAN COUNTY

Created: February 26, 1848, out of Henderson County. This region originally was a part of the Municipality of Nacogdoches.

Organized: August 7, 1848. An election in 1851 defined a permanent site for the county seat. By legislative edict, Kingsborough was chosen, but later the town was renamed Kaufman.

Named: For David Spangler Kaufman, who moved from Pennsylvania to Nachitoches, Louisiana. He later served in the Congress of the Republic and in other Texas government positions. David Kaufman was a charter member of the Philosophical Society of Texas.

MEDINA COUNTY

Created: February 12, 1848, from the Bexar District. Medina County was never subdivided.

Organized: August 7, 1848, with Castroville serving as the county seat. In 1892, the Southern Pacific Railroad asked Castroville for a bonus in exchange for routing its rail line through the city. The town refused. Consequently the line was routed south of town through Hondo, which then became the county seat.

Boundaries: By a legislative act of 1873, a part of Bexar County was annexed to enlarge Medina County.

Named: For the Medina River, which traverses the northeastern corner of the county. The river was named by Alonzo de León, who crossed it in 1689, after a Spanish engineer named Pedro Medina, whose navigation tables de León used. The original Spanish name can be traced back to the Moors.

STARR COUNTY

Created: From Nueces County on February 10, 1848.

Organized: August, 7, 1848. The creating act spelled out the name for the county seat: Rio Grande City.

Named: For Dr. James Harper Starr, who was born in Connecticut but migrated to Texas in 1837. Starr served the Republic of Texas as treasury secretary under President Lamar and then took an active role in the government of the Confederacy.

VAN ZANDT COUNTY

Created: From Henderson County on February 5, 1848.

Organized: July 13, 1846, with Sabine Lake selected as the county seat. Two years later, when Wood County was formed out of Van Zandt County, the county offices were moved to Canton. Construction of the Texas and Pacific Railroad in 1872 led to the establishment of a new town, Wills Point, and ignited a war over the county seat. Feeling that they had outgrown Canton, the citizens of Wills Point won an election to gain the county seat. Claiming fraud, the Wills Point people took up arms to recover the county records and government. Gov. R. B. Hubbard called out the state militia to keep peace until the matter could be settled. The state supreme court ruled in Canton's favor.

Named: For Issac Van Zandt, born in Tennessee in 1813 and who migrated to Texas in 1839. After attending the Constitutional Convention of 1845 which wrote the first state constitution, he served in several civic posts. Stricken with yellow fever, he died on October 11, 1847.

WEBB COUNTY

Created: January 28, 1848, from Bexar and Nueces counties in an attempt to control the region between the Nueces River and the Rio Grande.

Organized: March 16, 1848. Although located far from the center of the county, Laredo was a natural choice for county seat and has retained this position. Prior to the formation of Webb County, most of the residents considered themselves citizens of the Mexican state of Tamaulipas. They were not sympathetic toward the Texas revolutionaries; in fact, they held a ball for Santa Ana in 1836 as he traveled towards Bexar. After the Mexican-American War and pacification of the Nueces strip, local sympathies gradually changed.

Named: For James Webb, originally of Virginia, who served the Republic of Texas as attorney general, secretary of state, secretary of the treasury, and senator.

WILLIAMSON COUNTY

Created: March 13, 1848, out of Milam County. This area was in the Robertson Colony during Mexican rule.

Organized: August 7, 1848, when Georgetown was made county seat.

Named: For Maj. Robert M. Williamson, a Georgia native who was crippled for life but managed with a wooden leg that earned him the nickname "Three-Legged Willie." Trained as a lawyer, he came to Texas in 1828. Fluent in Spanish, he earned respect as an expert on the Mexican land laws that applied in Texas. After the Texas Revolution, Williamson served in the Congress of the Republic of Texas and in the first Texas Legislature.

1849 Additions: Map 5-10

ELLIS COUNTY

Created: Out of Navarro County on December 20, 1849. Ellis County had its beginning in the Department of Nacogdoches and in the Municipality of Milam during Mexican rule. In the 1840s, the northern part of the present county fell within Peters' Colony. The remainder was part of the Mercer Colony.

Organized: August 5, 1850, with Waxahachie as the county seat.

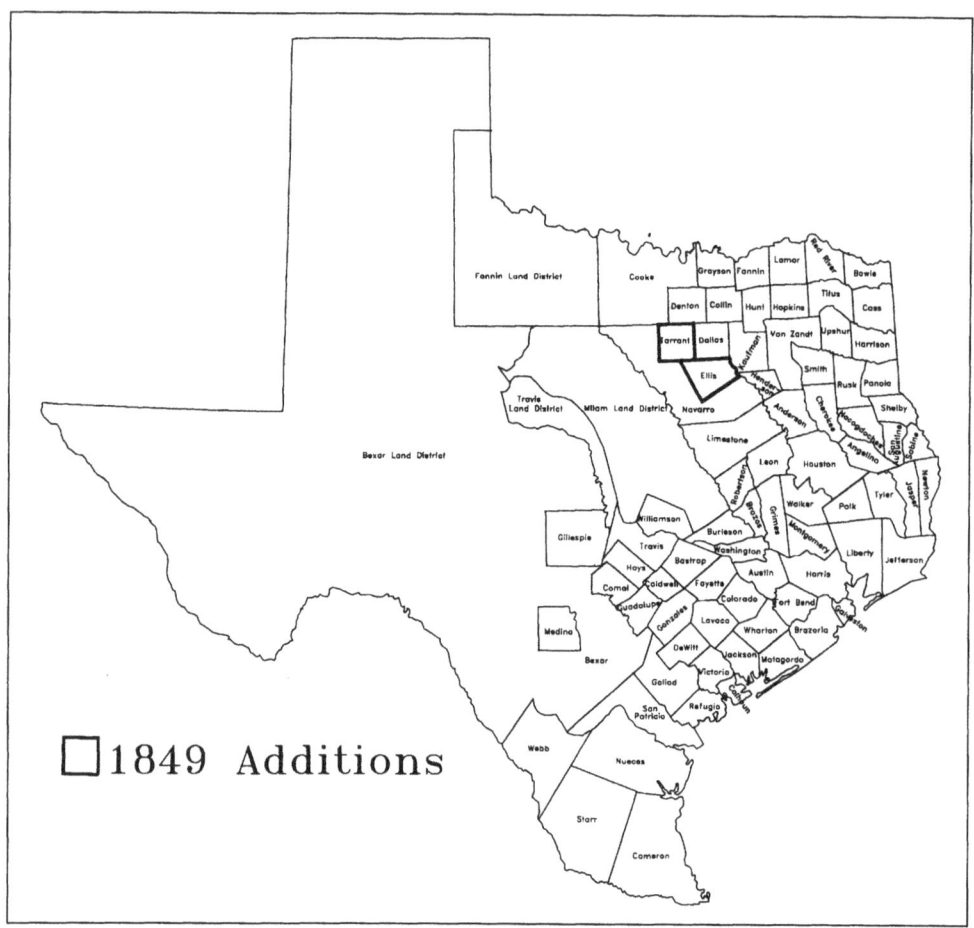

MAP 5-10. Changes in Texas counties, 1849. Map by Luke Gournay.

Named: For Richard Ellis, a Virginian who practiced law in Alabama. He framed the first state constitution of Alabama and served as a judge in that state. In 1825, he moved to the Red River area of Texas and began planting cotton on a large scale. Ellis was chosen as a delegate to the convention that declared Texas independent in 1836, then helped to frame the Constitution of the Republic. After Texas won its independence, Ellis was elected to the Congress of the Republic of Texas.

TARRANT COUNTY

Created: From part of Navarro County on December 20, 1849.
Organized: August 5, 1850. The first colonists established Bird's Fort, which was renamed Birdville and made the first county seat. In 1856, Fort Worth, now larger than Birdville, contested the designation of county seat, caus-

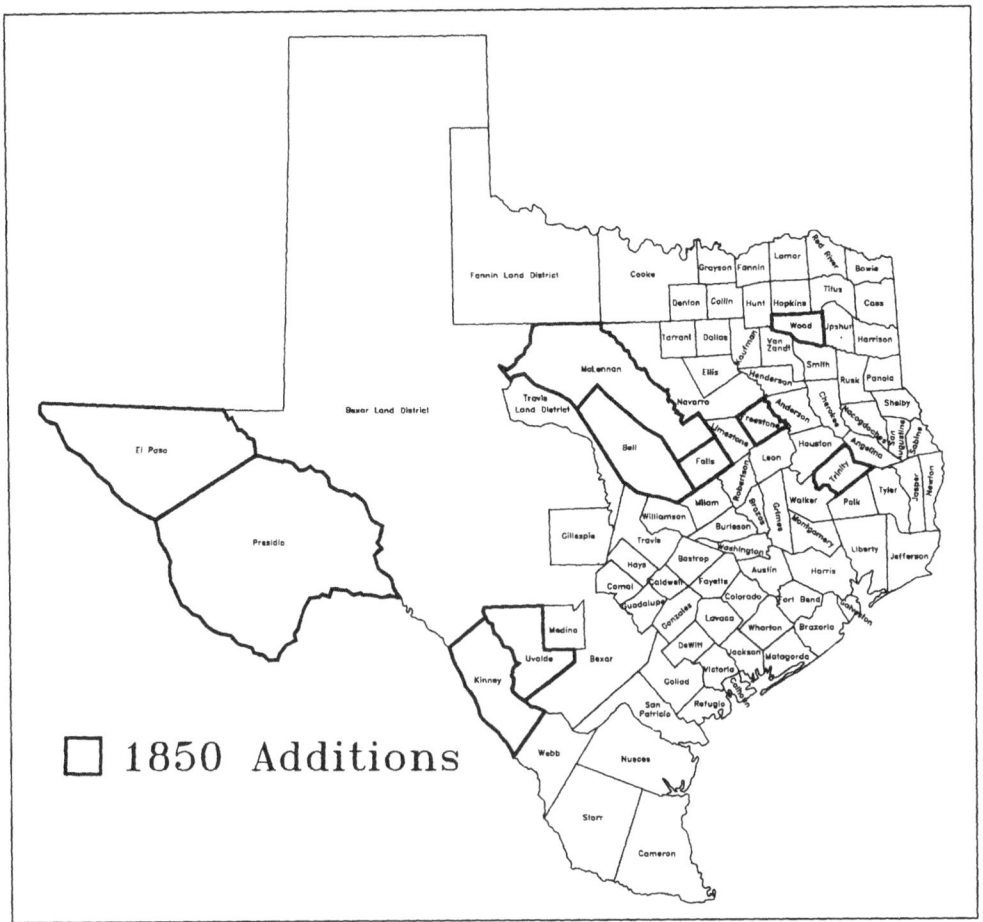

MAP 5-11. Changes in Texas counties, 1850. Map by Luke Gournay.

ing a new election to be held. Fort Worth won, capturing the county seat. Birdville initiated a second election in 1860, but Fort Worth won again. It has been county seat since.

Named: For General E. H. Tarrant, who came to Texas from Tennessee in 1835. He served in the Texas army near the end of the campaign for independence and served in the Texas Legislature after Texas became a state.

1850 Additions: Map 5-11

BELL COUNTY

Created: January 22, 1850, from Milam County. The area of Bell County was originally part of the Robertson Colony.

Organized: August 1, 1850. The first county seat was Nolan Springs, later named Nolanville. The name was changed again on December 16, 1851, this time to Belton.

Boundaries: A boundary change occurred in 1856, when a six-mile strip was transferred from Falls County to Bell County.

Named: For Peter H. Bell, a Virginian who arrived in Texas in April 1836. He joined Sam Houston at San Jacinto, served in the regular army, and twice became governor of the state. The ravages of the Civil War, which Bell had opposed, destroyed his fortune. Poverty marked the remainder of his life.

EL PASO COUNTY

Created: January 3, 1850, from Santa Fe County when that county was divided into Santa Fe, Worth, El Paso, and Presidio counties.

Organized: March 7, 1871, with the first county seat at San Elizario. The county government was moved to Ysleta in 1866, remaining there for two years. In 1868, it was moved back to Elizario, where it stayed until 1873. In that year, after another election, Ysleta regained its position as county seat. Once more, the railroads changed history. The rail line reached El Paso in 1881, bringing with it settlers, and El Paso became the county seat in 1883.

Named: For the Franklin Mountain pass in the Rocky Mountain chain. This was the first geographical name applied by the Spaniards to any part of Texas. Because of its particular location, all routes converge here, and in modern times all railways in that region meet in El Paso.

FALLS COUNTY

Created: January 28, 1850, from Milam County and a small part of Limestone County.

Organized: August 5, 1850, with Old Viesca initially designated as the county seat. That choice displeased many of the residents, and, after loud debate, Adams became the county seat on September 4, 1850. Adams, renamed Marlin, has retained that position.

Boundaries: A strip of land six miles wide along Elm Creek was removed from Falls County and attached to Bell County in 1856. The boundary between Falls and Limestone counties was adjusted in 1863.

Named: For a small waterfall on the Brazos.

FREESTONE COUNTY

Created: From Limestone County on September 6, 1850.

Organized: July 6, 1851, with Fairfield as the county seat.

Named: For the large difference in soil formation, compared to the abundant limestone in its parent county.

Created: January 28, 1850, out of the Bexar Land District. Beales and Grant started a colony here with fifty-nine colonists.
Organized: February 7, 1874, after Oscar B. Brackett was appointed to organize the county. The stage stop, Brackett, renamed Brackettville, was made the county seat.
Named: For Henry Lawrence Kinney, who came from Pennsylvania in 1838. Noted for founding Corpus Christi, Kinney served several terms in the Texas Legislature.

MCLENNAN COUNTY

Created: January 22, 1850, out of Milam, Limestone, and Navarro counties.
Organized: August 5, 1850, with Waco chosen as the county seat.
Named: For Neil McLennan, a Scotsman from North Carolina, who arrived by schooner in 1835. He settled on Pond Creek in present Falls County. While on a surveying trip, McLennan discovered the Bosque Valley, became enchanted with it, and resettled there. George Erath began surveying the territory in 1840 and laid out the town of Waco in 1849. In 1856, George Barnard opened a new store and trading post in Waco and settled there permanently.

PRESIDIO COUNTY

Created: January 3, 1850, from the Bexar Land District.
Organized: Partially in 1858; the town of Presidio del Norte was to be county seat. Full organization had to wait until 1875, when Fort Davis was made the seat of justice. Ten years later, in 1885, Marfa became the county seat.
Named: For the fortress that was erected across the Rio Grande to protect the Spanish missions.

TRINITY COUNTY

Created: Out of Houston County on February 11, 1850.
Organized: April 1, 1850. Sumpter, the home of John Wesley Hardin, was the first county seat and held that position for twenty-two years. Sumpter lost its position as county seat to Trinity on May 30, 1873, when the International–Great Northern Railroad built into Trinity. Sumpter turned into a ghost town. The seat of government moved to Pennington in 1874 and remained there for nine years. When the Pennington courthouse burned in 1883, the county commissioners held an election to choose a new county seat closer to the county's center. Groveton won this election and has been the base of government since.

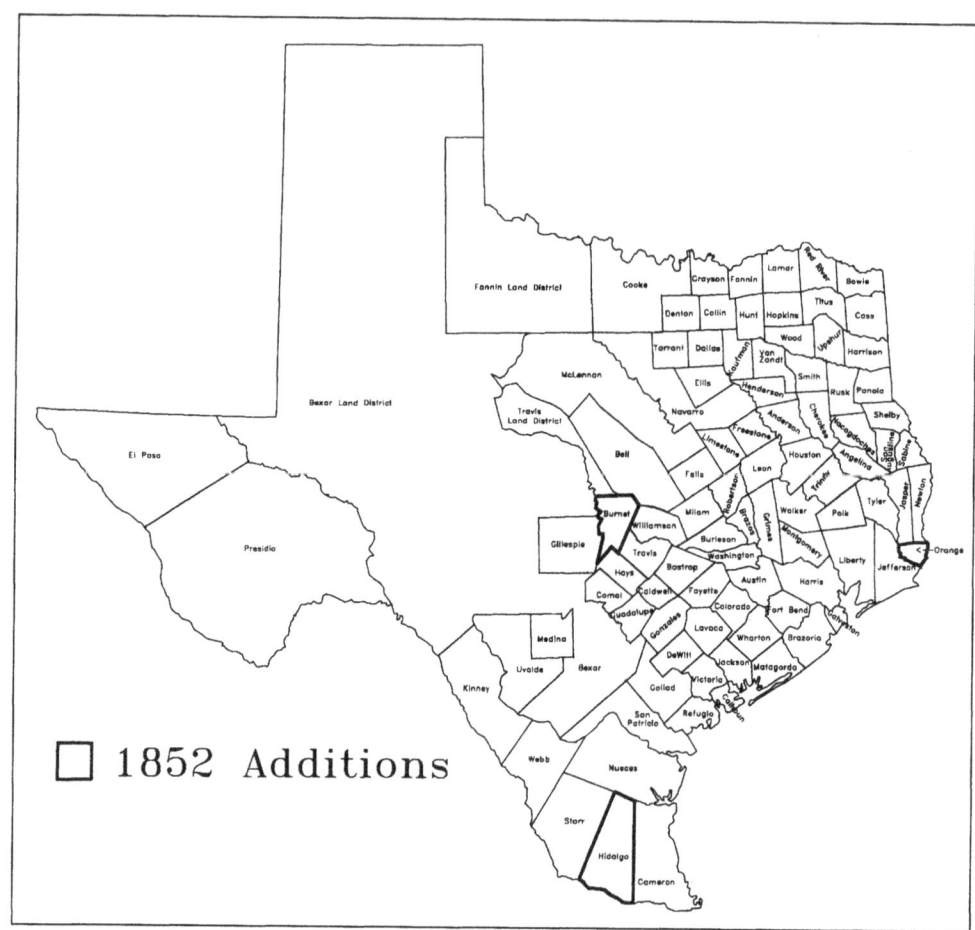

MAP 5-12. Changes in Texas counties, 1852. Map by Luke Gournay.

UVALDE COUNTY

Created: February 8, 1850, out of Bexar County.
Organized: April 21, 1856, with the town of Uvalde named county seat.
Named: For Uvalde Canyon. This natural feature was so titled in honor of the military governor of Coahuila and Texas in 1778, Juan de Uvalde.

WOOD COUNTY

Created: Out of Van Zandt County on February 5, 1850.
Organized: August 5, 1850, with Quitman chosen as the county seat. The town was named for a New York financier, John A. Quitman, who led a group of volunteers to fight for Texas' cause during the revolution.
Named: For George T. Wood, a Georgian who came to Texas in 1838 to

ranch. After serving in the Mexican-American War, Wood was active in the politics of the Republic of Texas and later of the state.

1852 Additions: Map 5-12

BURNET COUNTY

Created: From Bell, Travis, and Williamson counties on February 5, 1852.
Organized: August 7, 1854, with the town of Hamilton chosen as county seat. The legislature changed the name of Hamilton to Burnet in 1858.
Named: For David Gouverneur Burnet. Coming to Texas from New Jersey in 1826, he became an empresario under the Mexican government. Burnet was a member of the Consultation and served the Republic of Texas as interim president in 1836 and vice president in 1838.

HIDALGO COUNTY

One of the major Spanish settlements here was called Habitación. A Scottish investor acquired land in the area and changed the name of this community to Edinburg in 1852.
Created: January 24, 1852, from Cameron County.
Organized: August 7, 1852, when Edinburg was named the county seat. In 1885, the legislature changed the town's name to Hidalgo. This town of Hidalgo was moved from its original site to a new one and renamed Edinburg in 1911.
Named: For the patriot priest Padre Miguel Hidalgo, who launched the revolution to free Mexico from Spain in 1810. He was defeated, captured, and executed at Chihuahua in 1811. His head was severed from his body and prominently displayed by the royalists while his body was interred in Chihuahua. In 1823, after the Mexican Revolution, the body and its skull were transferred to the Chapel las Reyes, in the Cathedral of the City of Mexico. Here, he was reburied with the Viceroys and later the Presidents of the Republic of Mexico.

ORANGE COUNTY

Created: From Jefferson County on February 5, 1852.
Organized: March 20, 1852, when Madison was named the county seat. In a name-changing exercise, the legislature acted on five counties in 1858, and the town of Madison was renamed Orange.
Named: By George A. Patillo, who had an orange grove on the nearby Neches River.

1853 Additions: Map 5-13

HILL COUNTY

Created: February 7, 1853, out of Navarro County.
Organized: May 14, 1853. Three small communities competed for the county

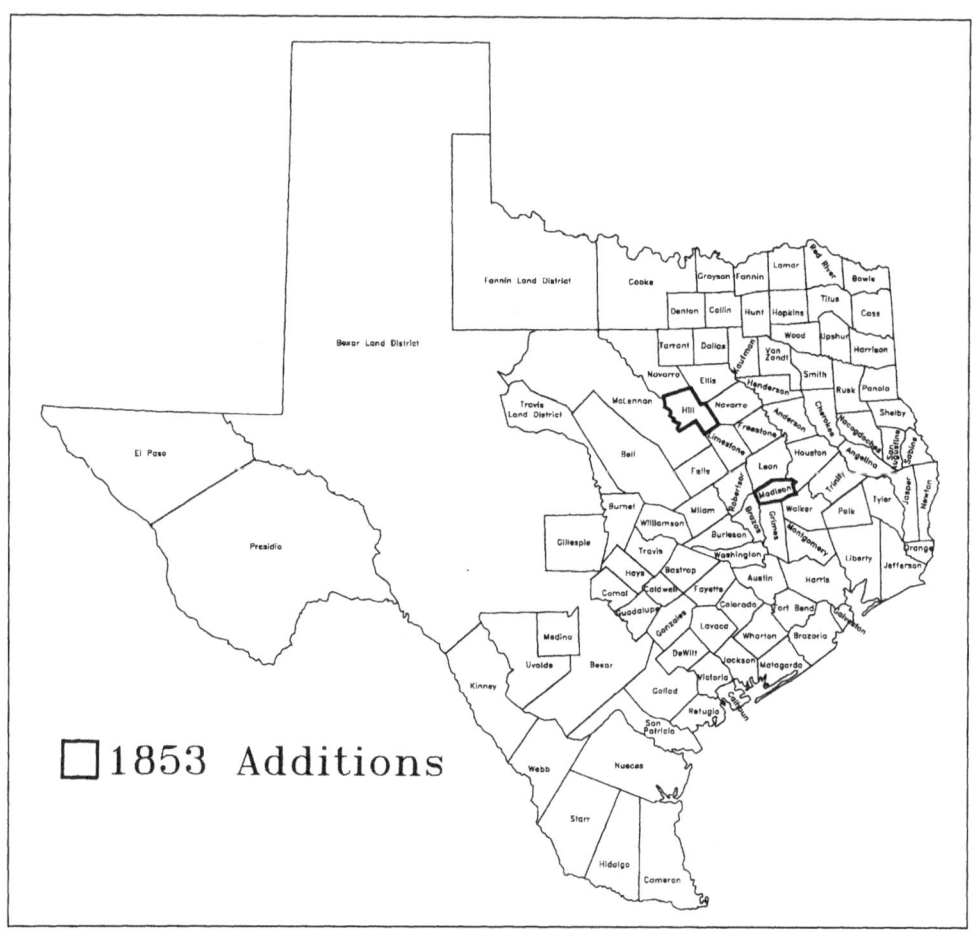

MAP 5-13. Changes in Texas counties, 1853. Map by Luke Gournay.

seat, but Hillsborough won on May 14, 1853. The name was shortened to Hillsboro.

Boundaries: In 1881, 5,334 acres were detached from Hill County and attached to Johnson County.

Named: For a Tennessee physician, Dr. George W. Hill. At the age of twenty-three, he came to Texas and settled in what is now Navarro County. Dr. Hill was elected to the Congress of the Republic a number of times. He was appointed secretary of war by Texas President Sam Houston, serving until the annexation. He was elected to the Texas Legislature several times.

MADISON COUNTY

Created: From Grimes, Walker, and Leon counties on January 27, 1853.
Organized: August 7, 1854, with Madisonville selected as county seat. The

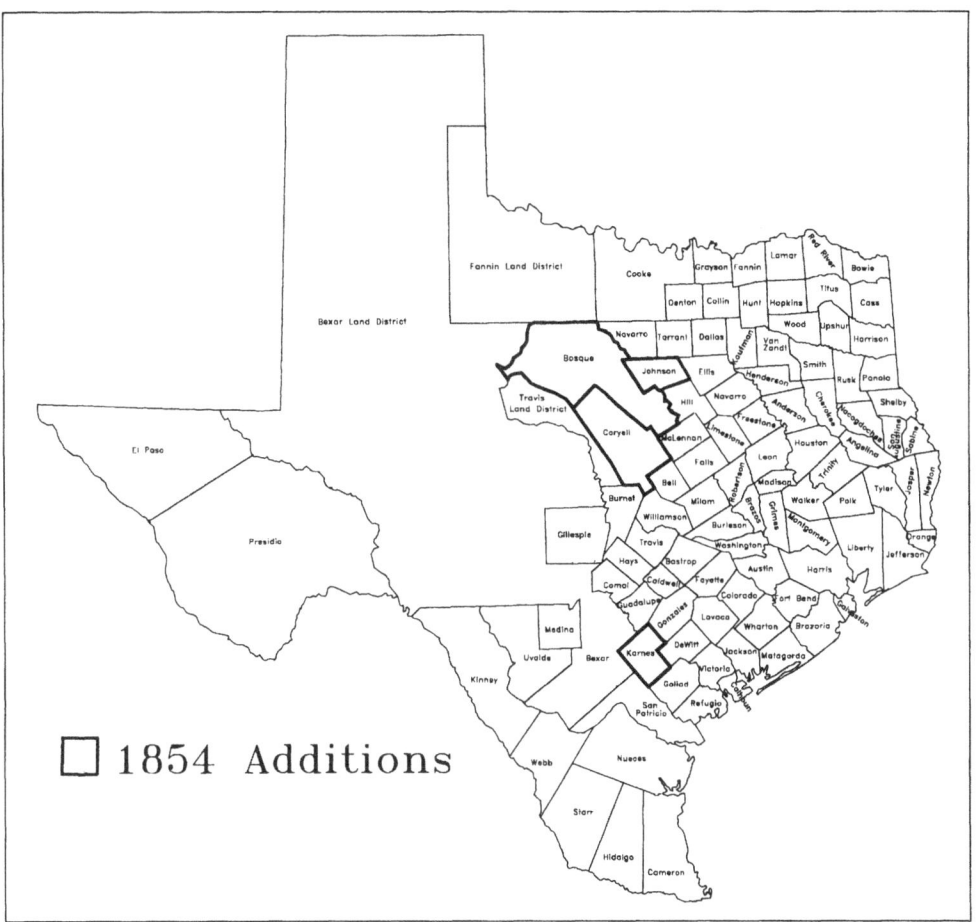

MAP 5-14. Changes in Texas counties, 1854. Map by Luke Gournay.

name was shortened to Madison in 1858. P. W. Kittrell was the leader in the organization process and became its first representative to the Texas Legislature.

Named: For President James Madison.

1854 Additions: Map 5-14

BOSQUE COUNTY

Created: February 4, 1854, out of Milam and McLennan counties. The area of present Bosque County was originally in Robertson Colony and later fell in the Milam Land District.

Organized: August 7, 1854. Meridian was made county seat.

Named: For the Bosque River. That name, meaning *forest* or *woody*, was given by Spanish explorers.

CORYELL COUNTY

Created: From Bell County on February 11, 1854.
Organized: March 11, 1854, when Gatesville was made the county seat.
Named: For James Coryell, who came from Tennessee in 1828, looking for the old San Saba River silver mines. He was unsuccessful and later settled in the present Bosque County area.

JOHNSON COUNTY

Created: February 4, 1854, out of Navarro and McLennan counties. This county was originally in the Robertson Colony. It was part of both Peters Colony and Mercer Colony while the Republic of Texas existed.
Organized: August 7, 1854, but a controversy erupted over location of the county seat. In a special election held in August 1855, Wardville won. A second election in 1856 determined that Wardville was not near enough to the center of the county. Two months later, the county seat was relocated to a site called Buchanan. Buchanan remained the county seat until November 1866, when Hood County was created. Since Hood's creation took the western portion of Johnson County, Buchanan was no longer in the geographical center of its county. In another election, held in March 1867, Camp Henderson became the new county seat. It was renamed Cleburne in honor of Patrick Cleburne, a Confederate general.
Boundaries: In March 1881, an area along the Brazos River was added to Johnson County from Hill County.
Named: For Middleton T. Johnson. Born in South Carolina, he located in Shelby County, Texas, in 1839. He served honorably as a Texas Ranger, legislator, and Confederate soldier.

KARNES COUNTY

Created: February 4, 1854, out of Bexar and Goliad counties.
Organized: February 27, 1854, when Helena, formerly Alamita, was chosen the county seat. In 1885, Helena was bypassed by the San Antonio and Aransas Pass Railroad. Instead, the line came through a point that was successively called St. Joe, Cestahowa, and Karnes City. Karnes City became the county seat in 1894.
Named: For Henry Racks Karnes, a Tennessean who moved to Texas in 1835. A participant in the siege of Bexar, he went on to the Battle of San Jacinto. After that battle, Karnes was sent to Matamoros to exchange prisoners. The Mexicans captured him there and placed him in prison. He escaped, only to die later of yellow fever.

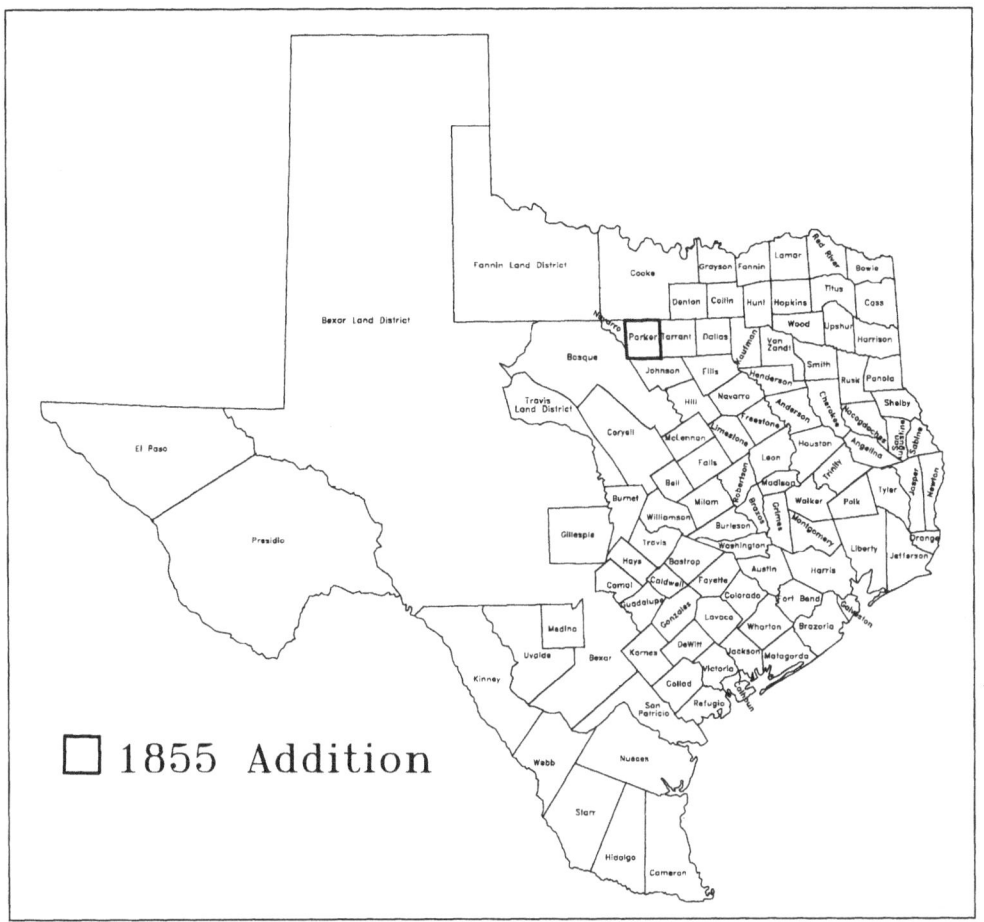

MAP 5-15. Changes in Texas counties, 1855. Map by Luke Gournay.

1855 Addition: Map 5-15

PARKER COUNTY

Created: December 2, 1855, from Bosque and Navarro counties.
Organized: March 11, 1856. The town of Weatherford was selected as county seat.
Named: For Isaac Parker, a representative of the Tarrant District in the Third, Fourth, Sixth, and Seventh congresses of the Republic of Texas. The county seat was named for Jefferson Weatherford, senator from the Dallas District.

Some of the present county fell inside the Austin and Williams grant, but no settlements developed during that period. By 1849, people began moving in and establishing communities. Dan Waggoner, one of the first settlers,

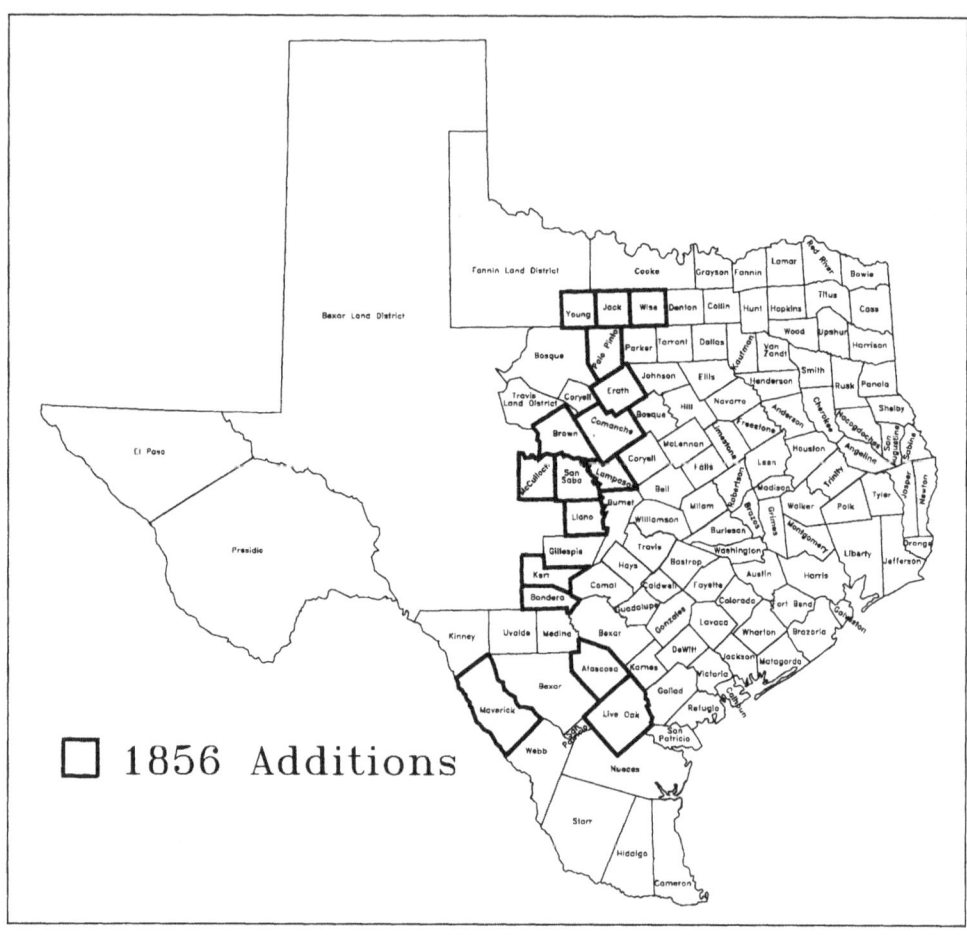

MAP 5-16. Changes in Texas counties, 1856. Map by Luke Gournay.

developed the largest ranch in this part of Texas. The Parker County area also attracted Oliver Loving, who, with Charles Goodnight, established the Goodnight-Loving Trail (see also 1887 Additions, Loving County).

1856 Additions: Map 5-16

ATASCOSA COUNTY

Created: From a section of Bexar Land District on January 25, 1856.
Organized: August 4, 1856, when Navatasco became the first county seat. The first courthouse was built on land donated by José Antonio Navarro. Competition for the county seat developed in 1858, when John Brown donated land for a new seat in Pleasanton (formerly Bonito Settlement). Pleasanton won, and the courts moved. The struggle for possession of

county government offices was renewed in 1908, when a businessman in Jourdanton developed a ninety-thousand-acre tract of land, offering every other tract to the San Antonio, Uvalde, and Gulf Railroad. The new town developed rapidly by 1909, when Jourdanton wrestled the designation as county seat from Pleasanton.

Named: From the Spanish word for *boggy*, after some explorers were caught in quicksand.

BANDERA COUNTY

Created: As another offspring of Bexar Land District, on January 25, 1856.
Organized: March 10, 1856. Bandera was chosen as county seat.
Named: For the Bandera Mountains in the northern part of the county.

BROWN COUNTY

Created: August 27, 1856, out of Comanche and Travis counties.
Organized: March 2, 1857. Brownwood was chosen as county seat.
Named: For Henry S. Brown, a Kentuckian who came to Texas in 1825. Joining a battle company, Brown was in command at the Battle of Velasco. He was an active participant in the Convention of 1832.

COMANCHE COUNTY

Created: January 25, 1856, from Bosque and Coryell counties.
Organized: March 17, 1856. Cora was the county seat until 1859, when Comanche, ten miles away, was selected because of its more central location.
Named: For the Comanche Indians.

ERATH COUNTY

Created: January 25, 1856, from parts of Bosque and Coryell counties.
Organized: August 4, 1856, when Stephenville was chosen as county seat.
Boundaries: Erath County lines were modified in 1856 and in 1860.
Named: For George B. Erath, who was born and educated in Vienna, Austria. Arriving in the United States in 1832, he became a surveyor in Robertson County. Erath fought in the Battle of San Jacinto and later served in various military units. Afterward, he formed a company of surveyors and planned the city of Waco in 1849. Much of his career was spent in the Congress of the Republic of Texas and in the Texas Legislature and the Texas Senate.

JACK COUNTY

Created: August 27, 1856, out of Cook County.
Organized: July 1, 1857. The first center of government was in Lost Creek. Lost Creek was renamed twice: first Mesquiteville, then Jacksborough in

1858. When the name was shortened to Jacksboro in 1899, the postmaster of Jacksborough had to resign and be reappointed postmaster of Jacksboro.

Named: For William H. and Patrick C. Jack, who came to Texas from North Carolina by way of Alabama. The brothers ended up in the midst of the uprisings at Anahuac, where Patrick had been imprisoned by the Mexicans. Later, they both held important posts in the Republic of Texas and the Texas state government.

KERR COUNTY

Created: January 25, 1856, from Bexar County.

Organized: March 22, 1856, when Kerrville was made county seat. In 1860, Comfort became the center of justice. When Kendall County was created in 1862, Comfort became part of Kendall County, and Kerrville again became the county seat.

Named: For James Kerr, a Kentucky lawyer who came to Texas in 1825 to manage DeWitt's colony. Soon after arriving, he lost his wife and two children but continued his duties. He laid out the town of Gonzales in 1826 and prepared it for settlers. Kerr was a member of the Conventions of 1832 and 1833 and attended the Consultation in 1835, and the Constitutional Convention in 1836. He served in the Third Congress of the Republic of Texas.

LAMPASAS COUNTY

Created: February 1, 1856, from parts of Travis and Bell counties.

Organized: March 10, 1856, with Burleson recognized as the county seat. The town's name was changed to Lampasas, which means *lilies* in Spanish. But lilies are not native to this area, so it is presumed that the name accidentally was exchanged with that of the Salado (salty) River. The error was never corrected.

LIVE OAK COUNTY

Created: February 12, 1856, from parts of Nueces and San Patricio counties.

Organized: August 4, 1856. Oakville became the first county seat. When the San Antonio, Uvalde, and Gulf Railroad was built in 1919, it missed Oakville, passing through George West instead. Consequently, George West, which was named after its founder, became county seat.

Named: For the beginning of the live oak belt that grows at the end of the extensive post oak belt.

LLANO COUNTY

Created: From parts of Bexar and Gillespie counties on August 4, 1856.

Organized: August 4, 1856, when the town of Llano was selected as the county seat.

Named: For the Spanish geographical term designating the landform of a plain. The river of the same name flows through the city and empties into the Colorado River.

The region was first mapped in 1847 by Ferdinand von Roemer, a fact that suggests the great variety of people who were attracted to Texas. Von Roemer had studied law at Göttingen, Germany, but earned a Ph.D. degree in paleontology in Berlin in 1842. He came to Texas shortly thereafter, exploring a large area. After studying the flora and fauna, Roemer wrote a book entitled *Texas*, published in Bonn, Germany, in 1849. He also published the first learned paper on Texas geology, "The Cretaceous Formations of Texas and Their Organic Inclusions."

MAVERICK COUNTY

Created: February 2, 1856, from Kinney County.
Organized: July 13, 1871, with Eagle Pass designated as county seat.
Named: For Samuel Augustus Maverick, a Yale graduate from South Carolina who migrated to Texas in 1835. He arrived just in time to participate in the Texas Revolution. The Mexicans arrested him in October 1835 and held him in San Antonio until he escaped. Maverick then assisted Ben Milam in storming and taking the presidio. He was a framer of the Texas Declaration of Independence in 1836. Captured by General Woll during a raid into Texas in 1842, Maverick was held in chains in Mexico and forced to labor on a road gang. After his release in 1845, he served in the Texas Legislature.

MCCULLOCH COUNTY

Created: As another product of Bexar County, on August 27, 1856.
Organized: 1876, with Brady City, now known as Brady, as the county seat.
Named: For Ben McCulloch. He came from Tennessee in 1835, an opportune time to join the fight for independence. In charge of the two brass cannons at San Jacinto, McCulloch was recognized for bravery. He served in the Congress of the Republic of Texas; was a successful Indian scout, Texas Ranger, and scout in the Mexican-American War; became sheriff of Sacramento County in California and United States marshal in 1853; and saw action in the Confederate army. He had attained the rank of brigadier general when he was killed on March 7, 1862. He was buried with honors in the Texas State Cemetery at Austin.

PALO PINTO COUNTY

Created: From Bosque and Navarro counties on August 27, 1856.
Organized: April 27, 1857, with the town of Golconda picked as county seat. That name was changed to Palo Pinto in the following year to match the Palo Pinto Creek that traverses the county.

Boundaries: The legislature modified the boundaries of Palo Pinto, Erath, and Johnson counties in 1866.

SAN SABA COUNTY

Created: From the Bexar District on February 1, 1856.
Organized: May 3, 1856, with Rowe's Land named the county seat. After a special election on July 19, 1856, the county seat was moved from Rowe's Land to San Saba.
Named: For the San Saba River. The belief is that Spanish missionaries found the river on a Saturday (*sábado*) and, according to custom, named it Holy Saturday or San Sabado.

WISE COUNTY

Created: From a part of Cooke County on January 23, 1856.
Organized: May 5, 1856, when Bishop's Hill was chosen as county seat. The town was renamed Taylorsville and then Decatur in 1857, in recognition of Stephen Decatur, a commodore in the American Revolution.
Named: For a man who was an advocate for Texas but never saw the land: Henry A. Wise, a lawyer from Virginia. He was a professional politician who served in political positions during his entire career. Wise championed the cause of Texas in the United States Congress and strongly advocated annexation.

YOUNG COUNTY

Created: February 2, 1856, from Bosque and Fannin counties. The creating act also stipulated that a large area to the west, extending to New Mexico, would be named Young Territory. In 1874, part of Young County was made a land district.
Organized: 1856, with Belknap chosen to be the county seat. The Civil War had encouraged renewed Indian attacks, causing a long delay in organization. During this period, county records were stored in Jacksboro for safekeeping, while Wise County served judicial needs. A second organization took place on April 17, 1874, with Graham selected as county seat.
Named: For William Cocke Young, who was a delegate to the first State Constitutional Convention and afterward served in the Texas Legislature.

1857 Additions: Map 5-17

BEE COUNTY

Created: December 8, 1857, from portions of five existing counties: San Patricio, Goliad, Refugio, Live Oak, and Karnes.
Organized: January 25, 1858, with a courthouse at Beeville on Medio Creek.

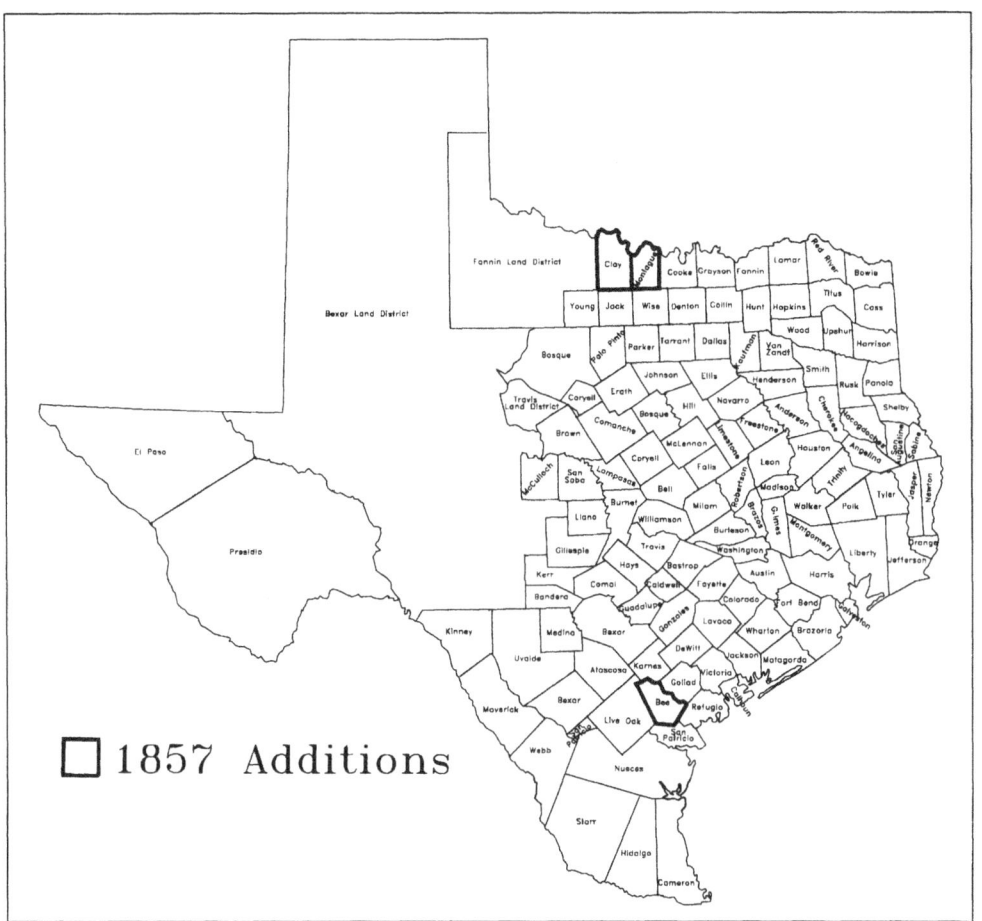

MAP 5-17. Changes in Texas counties, 1857. Map by Luke Gournay.

In 1860, the courthouse was moved to Maryville, later called Beeville-on-the-Poesta. Today, the town is known simply as Beeville.

Named: For Barnard E. Bee, a North Carolinian who came to Texas in 1836 and volunteered in the Texas army. Bee was one of three commissioners who accompanied Santa Ana to Washington, D.C., after the Battle of San Jacinto.

CLAY COUNTY

Created: From Cooke County on December 24, 1857.

Organized: Unsuccessfully in 1860. This attempt had to be set aside because of the Civil War. On May 27, 1873, the county was reorganized. Henrietta, formerly Cambridge, was named the county seat to comply with the legislative creating act.

Named: For Henry Clay, the illustrious Virginian who spent many productive years in the United States House of Representatives and Senate.

MONTAGUE COUNTY

Created: From Cooke County on December 24, 1857.
Organized: August 2, 1858, with the town of Montague named as county seat.
Boundaries: The county line was modified in 1879.
Named: For Daniel Montague, who came to Texas from Massachusetts in 1836, settling in the present Fannin County. A professional surveyor, Montague took time to fight in the Mexican-American War. By locating land certificates in the great Fannin Land District, Montague accumulated large personal landholdings. After the Civil War, he joined other prominent Texas citizens who fled to Mexico.

1858 Additions: Map 5-18

In one legislative act on January 22, 1858, eight counties came into existence. These counties were: Archer, Buchanan, Hamilton, Hardin, Kimble, Mason, Menard, and Zapata. A seat of government was named for each.

On February 1, 1858, the Texas Legislature busied itself with the creation of another group of counties: Baylor, Callahan, Coleman, Concho, Dawson, Dimmit, Duval, Eastland, Edwards, Encinal, Frio, Hardeman, Haskell, Jones, Knox, La Salle, McMullen, Runnels, Shackelford, Taylor, Wichita, Wilbarger, and Zavala. This creating act also specified the county seats.

Dawson and Encinal can be sources of confusion, as neither appears on today's Texas map. The first Dawson County was created on February 1, 1858, but was never organized. A favorable climate for government did not develop, but the legislature never took concrete steps to abolish this county. It vanished in a de facto manner with the legislative acts of 1866 that restructured Kinney, Uvalde and Maverick counties. The first Dawson County is shown on the Texas maps for the period of its existence. A second Dawson County came into existence in 1876.

Encinal County was created out of present Webb County on February 1, 1856, but was never organized. The county was formally abolished on March 12, 1899, and the land was restored to Webb County. Encinal County is shown on the maps of Texas during the years of its existence.

ARCHER COUNTY

Created: From the Fannin Land District on January 22, 1858. Archer was first attached to Montague County for judicial purposes, then to Clay County.
Organized: July 27, 1880, with Archer City as county seat.

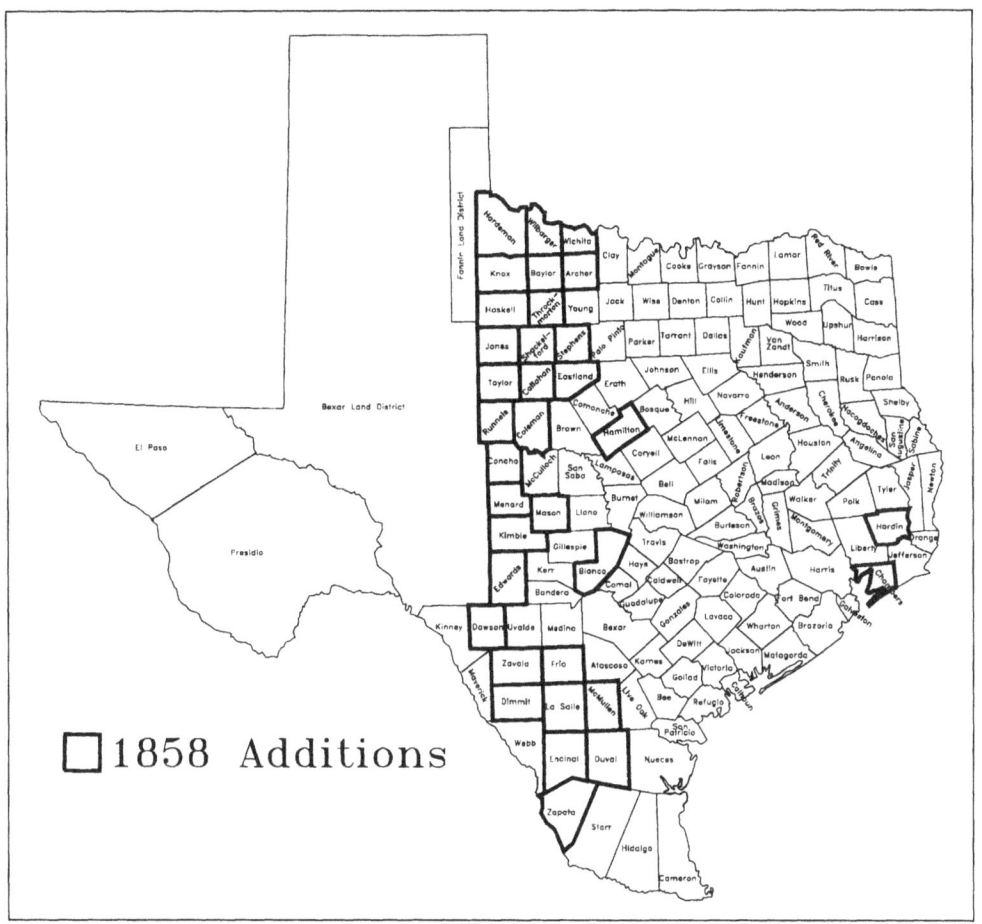

MAP 5-18. Changes in Texas counties, 1858. Map by Luke Gournay.

Named: For Branch Tanner Archer, an early Texas Revolutionary leader and member of the First Congress of the Republic of Texas. Archer was a medical doctor who came from Virginia and spent most of his adult life in southeastern Texas.

BAYLOR COUNTY

Created: From the Fannin Land District on February 1, 1858.
Organized: April 12, 1879. A courthouse was built in 1884 at the county seat of Seymour, after furious feuds between farmers and ranchers had been quelled.
Named: For Dr. Henry Weidner Baylor, a physician who migrated from Kentucky to LaGrange, Texas, where he set up his practice. Baylor volunteered to serve as a surgeon in the Mexican-American War.

Created: From parts of Burnet, Comal, Gillespie, and Hays counties, on February 12, 1858.
Organized: April 12, 1858, with Blanco designated as county seat. The divisive secession issue resulted in the formation of Kendall County out of the western part of Blanco County. After three bitterly fought elections, the county seat was moved to Johnson City from Blanco in 1891.
Named: By the legislature for the Blanco River. The Spanish *blanco* means *white*.

CALLAHAN COUNTY

Created: Out of Bexar, Travis, and Bosque counties on February 11, 1858.
Organized: July 3, 1877, with the town of Belle Plain as county seat. In 1880, when the Texas and Pacific Railroad came through, it missed Belle Plain. The line went through Baird, which became the seat of county government.
Named: For James Hughes Callahan, who came to Texas in 1835 with the Georgia Battalion. Callahan was taken prisoner at Coleto, but his life was spared because of his mechanical skills. He died in a personal fight in 1856.

CHAMBERS COUNTY

Created: From Liberty and Jefferson counties, February 12, 1858. This region was in the grants of empresarios Haden Edwards, Joseph Vehlein, David G. Burnet, and Lorenzo de Zavala.
Organized: August 2, 1858, with a county seat at Wallaceville. In 1908, a suit to move the county seat to Anahuac, formerly Perry's Point, was successful. Since Anahuac is not at the county's center, several attempts, all unsuccessful, were made to move the county government. At least four attempts were made to dissolve the county—in 1915, 1923, 1925, and 1931. In 1935, an oil discovery in the county put a stop to these threats.
Named: After a Virginian, Gen. Thomas Jefferson Chambers, who, in 1829, became surveyor general of Texas. A supporter of the Texas drive for independence, Chambers was active in public affairs until his death by assassination in 1865.

COLEMAN COUNTY

Created: From Brown and Travis counties, on February 1, 1858, and attached to Brown County for judicial purposes.
Organized: Initial organization took place on October 6, 1862, with Coleman as county seat. Court initially was held at a military post, Camp Colorado. The final county organization took place October 6, 1864.
Named: For Robert M. Coleman, who came to Texas from Kentucky in 1832. A member of the Consultation and the Convention of 1836, he signed

the Texas Declaration of Independence. Joining the army, Coleman was made an aide to Gen. Sam Houston.

CONCHO COUNTY

Created: From Bexar, on February 1, 1858. The county was initially attached to McCulloch County for judicial purposes.
Organized: March 11, 1879. Paint Rock was the first and only county seat.
Named: For the Concho River which, in turn, was named for the conch shells found in the river.

DIMMIT COUNTY

Created: From Bexar, Maverick, Uvalde, and Webb counties, on February 1, 1858.
Organized: November 2, 1880, with Carrizo Springs as county seat.
Named: After Phillip Dimmit, a Pennsylvanian who came to Texas in 1822. Dimmit strongly supported the cause of Texas independence, fighting with the troops at Goliad. Later, he and others were captured by Mexican raiders and taken to Monterrey for execution. Dimmit escaped but was recaptured. Preferring to die by his own hand, he wrote a letter to his wife giving directions for the disposal of his property, then took a lethal dose of opium.

DUVAL COUNTY

Created: February 1, 1858, from parts of Nueces, Live Oak, and Starr counties.
Organized: November 7, 1876, with San Diego as the county seat.
Boundaries: Attempts were made in 1913 and in 1915 to divide Duval County by the creation of Dunn and Lanham counties. Both efforts failed.
Named: For Captain Burr H. Duval, a Kentuckian who brought a company of volunteers to the mouth of the Brazos River in 1836. They joined Fannin's command in time to be captured and executed.

EASTLAND COUNTY

Created: Out of Bosque, Coryell, and Travis counties, on February 1, 1858. This territory was part of the Stephen Austin and Samuel Williams empresario grant.
Organized: December 2, 1873. A ranch headquarters called Merriman became the first county seat in February 1874. The county seat was moved to Eastland in 1875.
Named: For Thomas B. Eastland, who moved from Tennessee to LaGrange in 1834. Volunteering for the army, he fought at San Jacinto. In 1842, he organized a company to defend against General Woll in San Antonio. Captured in the Battle of Mier, he was executed in 1843.

EDWARDS COUNTY

Created: February 1, 1858, from the Bexar Land District.
Organized: April 10, 1883, with Leakey as the county seat. Leakey was replaced by Rock Springs in 1891.
Named: For Haden Edwards, who came from Kentucky in 1825. He obtained a grant from Mexico to bring eight hundred settlers into Texas. Conflicts arose within his colony that led to the annulment of his contract.

FRIO COUNTY

Created: From Atascosa, Bexar, and Uvalde counties, on February 1, 1858.
Organized: Partially on July 20, 1871, when Frio Town, the first town in the county, became the county seat. Indian attacks, which hampered settlement, continued until 1877. The International-Great Northern Railroad encouraged settlement but led to a loss for Frio Town. A station on the line, Pearsall, replaced Frio Town in 1883.
Named: For the Frio (cold) River.

HAMILTON COUNTY

Created: January 22, 1858, from parts of Comanche, Bosque, and Lampasas counties.
Organized: 1858, with Hamilton as county seat.
Named: For Gen. James Hamilton of South Carolina. While a United States congressman, he was appointed by Texas President Lamar to be a commercial and diplomatic agent for Texas in Europe. He negotiated favorable treaties of commerce and navigation with England and Holland. It wasn't until 1857 that he tried to reach Texas, but he died when his ship, the *Apolusis*, wrecked and sank.

HARDEMAN COUNTY

Created: February 21, 1858, from the Fannin Land District.
Organized: After second creation on December 1, 1884. The first county seat was the small town of Argurita, whose name was changed to Margaret. In 1885, the Fort Worth and Denver Railroad came through, creating a town at Quanah, named for Quanah Parker (Quanna Parker was the half-Indian, half-white son of Chief Peta Nocona and Naduah, the former Cynthia Ann Parker. Quanna grew up to become the last chief of the Comanche.) To Margaret's chagrin, some people wanted the county seat moved to Quanah. After establishing residence by having laundry done in town for six weeks, all the railroad crews became citizens and voted to make Quanah the seat of government.
Named: For two brothers, Bailey and Thomas Jones Hardeman, who came to Texas from Tennessee in 1835. Both took part in the revolution. Bailey

was a delegate to the Convention of 1836, and became secretary of the treasury under Texas President Burnet. Thomas Hardeman likewise entered the fight for independence and later served in various government positions.

HARDIN COUNTY

Created: January 22, 1858, out of the original counties of Jefferson and Liberty.
Organized: August 2, 1858, with the town of Hardin as first county seat. Once again, the coming of the railroad caused a political change. The Sabine and East Texas Railroad came into the county in 1880, missing Hardin. Adding to Hardin's problems, the courthouse burned. In 1887, the county seat was moved to Kountze. The town of Hardin is now known as "Old Hardin," to distinguish it from a town of the same name in Liberty County.
Named: For the Hardin family, who moved from Georgia to present Liberty County in 1825. The five brothers in the family served in several branches of the government.

HASKELL COUNTY

Created: February 1, 1858, from Milam and Fannin counties.
Organized: January 13, 1885, when Haskell, formerly Rice Springs, became the seat of justice.
Named: For Charles Ready Haskell. A native of Tennessee, he came to Texas and joined the revolution. Under James Fannin, Jr., Haskell fought in the Battle of Coleto. With Fannin's company, he was captured and executed by the Mexicans.

JONES COUNTY

Created: From Bexar County, on February 1, 1858. More than twenty years elapsed before any communities were established.
Organized: June 13, 1881, after being recreated in 1876. Jones City was chosen as county seat. In 1882, residents voted to change the name of the county seat to Anson.
Named: For Anson Jones, last president of the Republic of Texas. Jones presided over the lowering of the republic's flag and the raising of the United States flag.

KIMBLE COUNTY

Created: January 22, 1858, from the Bexar Land District. Kimble was attached to Gillespie County for judicial purposes until organized.
Organized: January 3, 1876, with Kimbleville as county seat. This town was moved and renamed Junction City. It became simply Junction in 1876.

Named: For George C. Kimbell, who responded to Travis' call for help at the Alamo. He died with the defenders. The name was misspelled when the county was created, but the error was never corrected.

KNOX COUNTY

Created: From the Fannin Land District, on February 1, 1858; attached to Baylor County for judicial needs.
Organized: March 20, 1886, with Benjamin as county seat.
Named: For Henry Knox, secretary of war under George Washington.

LA SALLE COUNTY

Created: February 1, 1858, out of the Bexar Land District.
Organized: November 2, 1880, with the first center of government at La Salle. In 1882, the town of Cotulla was established and became the new county seat.
Named: For the famous French explorer, René Robert Cavelier, Sieur de la Salle.

MCMULLEN COUNTY

Created: From Atascosa, Bexar, and Live Oak counties, on February 1, 1858.
Organized: Partially in 1862, but organization could not be completed. The county was reorganized in 1877, when Tilden became the county seat.
Named: For a well-educated Irishman, John C. McMullen, who started a business in Matamoros, Mexico, in the early 1820s but soon became interested in Texas colonization. With Patrick McGloin, later his son-in-law, McMullen became an empresario, obtaining a grant along the Nueces River in 1828. This venture became known as the McMullen-McGloin, or the Irish, Colony. Their grant covered the present counties of San Patricio, Bee, Karnes, Wilson, and Atascosa.

MASON COUNTY

Created: January 22, 1858, from Gillespie County and the Bexar Land District.
Organized: Partially on August 2, 1858. Mason won an election on May 22, 1861, to become the county seat.
Named: For Fort Mason, established in 1851 by Bvt. Maj. H. W. Merrill. It housed his command of the United States Dragoons. Lt. Col. Robert E. Lee was one of the famous officers who served here.

MENARD COUNTY

Created: January 22, 1858, from the Bexar Land District.
Organized: Partially in 1858, but organization was halted by Indian attacks.

Menardville, renamed Menard, became the county seat upon final organization on May 8, 1871.

Named: For a French Canadian, Col. Michel Branamour Menard. A fur trader and chief of a Shawnee tribe, he moved to Texas in 1833, establishing a trading business with the Mexicans and Indians near Nacogdoches. He participated in the Convention of 1836 and signed the Texas Declaration of Independence. In 1836, Colonel Menard purchased a league of barren land on Galveston Island for fifty thousand dollars. With partners, he established the City of Galveston. He represented Galveston in the Congress of the Republic of Texas and was a powerful figure in the government of the republic.

RUNNELS COUNTY

Created: From the Bexar Land District and Travis County on February 1, 1858.

Organized: February 16, 1880, with Runnels City, now Runnels, as county seat. Ballinger, established when the Gulf, Colorado, and Santa Fe Railroad was built, became the county seat in 1886.

Named: For Hiram G. Runnels, a Georgian who moved to Mississippi as a youngster. Adept at politics, he became governor of Mississippi in 1833. In 1836, while president of a bank, he caned the new governor in public and then fought a duel with the editor of the *Mississippian*. Probably as a result of these altercations, he moved to Texas in 1842, re-entering politics as a state representative for Brazoria and Galveston counties.

SHACKELFORD COUNTY

Created: From Bosque County, on February 1, 1858.

Organized: September 12, 1874. Although the legislature had specified that the county seat be named Shackleford (different spelling), voters chose Fort Griffin as county seat. Plans to abandon Fort Griffin led to the selection of Albany as the center of justice in 1875.

Named: For Dr. John Shackelford, a surgeon from Virginia and Alabama. Leaving all responsibilities behind and at his own expense, he formed a band of volunteers to join the Texas Revolution. Being uniformed in red jeans, his group was called the "Red Rovers." Their lives were cut short when they were captured with Fannin's troops and executed. Dr. Shackelford was spared so that the Mexicans could use his services. He escaped after the Battle of San Jacinto and returned to Alabama to practice medicine.

STEPHENS COUNTY

Created: From Bosque County, on January 22, 1858.

Organized: 1861, with Picketville chosen as a temporary county seat. The county was reorganized in 1876, at which time Breckenridge became the county seat.

Named: Buchanan originally, after the United States president. The county name was changed to Stephens in 1861, to honor Alexander H. Stephens, vice-president of the Confederacy.

TAYLOR COUNTY

Created: February 1, 1858, from parts of Bexar and Travis counties.

Organized: July 3, 1878, with Buffalo Gap as county seat. In 1880, the Texas and Pacific Railroad came through the northern part of the county. It missed Buffalo Gap and helped establish Abilene, which became county seat in 1881.

Named: For the Taylor family, members of the old Robertson Colony.

THROCKMORTON COUNTY

Created: From parts of Fannin and Bosque counties, on January 13, 1858.

Organized: March 18, 1879. Although the legislature meant for Williamsburg to be the county seat, Throckmorton was chosen. County court was held at Tarrant and Gibbons Ranch on Elm Creek until a building could be built.

Named: For Dr. William Edward Throckmorton of Virginia. Moving to Texas in 1841, he established a medical practice in the present Collin County area.

WICHITA COUNTY

Created: From the Fannin Land District on February 1, 1858. Attached to Clay County for judicial needs.

Organized: June 21, 1882, with the required 150 names on a petition for organization. It is suspected that many of these names belonged to transients and a few horses. Two sites vied to become county seat: Wichita Falls and the ranch house of Samuel Burk Burnett. Wichita Falls won by a narrow margin.

Named: Perhaps after Choctaw words for *big arbor,* or Comanche for *corn eater,* or Osage for *people with scattered camps.*

WILBARGER COUNTY

Created: From the Bexar Land District, on February 1, 1858. Attached to Clay County for judicial purposes.

Organized: October 10, 1881, when Vernon became the county seat.

Named: For Virginians Josiah Pugh Wilbarger and his brother Mathias Wilbarger. Arriving in Texas in 1829, they settled in the Bastrop area. Josiah Wilbarger was shot, scalped, and left for dead by Comanche Indians. He was found the next day, still alive, and managed to recover and live another twelve years.

Created: January 22, 1858, from parts of Webb and Starr counties.
Organized: April 26, 1858, with Carrizo (now Zapata) chosen to be county seat.
Named: For Col. Antonio Zapata, who led a small revolt against Santa Ana in the 1820s. With Gen. Antonio Canales, he established the Republic of the Rio Grande, which existed for a brief time before its capitulation. Colonel Zapata was captured and shot. His head was severed and stuck on a pole as a warning to other would-be revolutionaries.

ZAVALA COUNTY

Created: Out of Maverick and Kinney counties, on February 1, 1858. Zavala was attached, in turn, to the following counties for judicial purposes: Uvalde, Maverick, and Frio.
Organized: February 25, 1884, when Batesville, formerly known as Bates' Ditch, became the county seat. The San Antonio, Uvalde, and Gulf Railroad came to Crystal City in 1908. Rapid growth resulted in that city's becoming the county seat in 1928.
Named: For Lorenzo de Zavala, a Mexican revolutionary who agitated against Spain. Zavala was the first signer of the first Mexican Constitution. Disenchanted with Santa Ana, he moved to Texas in 1835, sympathizing with the oppressed Texans. Elected a member of the Consultation, Zavala helped to frame the Texas Constitution. On March 17, 1836, he was elected ad interim vice-president of the Republic of Texas, a position he held until October 17, 1836.

1860 Additions: Map 5-19

GREER COUNTY

The history of this county was touched on in chapter 4. The county is shown on the Texas map until its dissolution in 1896.

MARION COUNTY

Created: February 8, 1860, from Cass and Harrison counties.
Organized: March 16, 1860, with Jefferson, a port city, as county seat.
Boundaries: Adjustments were made in 1861 and 1863. On April 30, 1874, a portion of the county of Harrison was annexed to Marion County.
Named: After Gen. Francis Marion, who provided distinguished service during the American Revolutionary War. Marion did not venture to the Texas frontier in his lifetime.

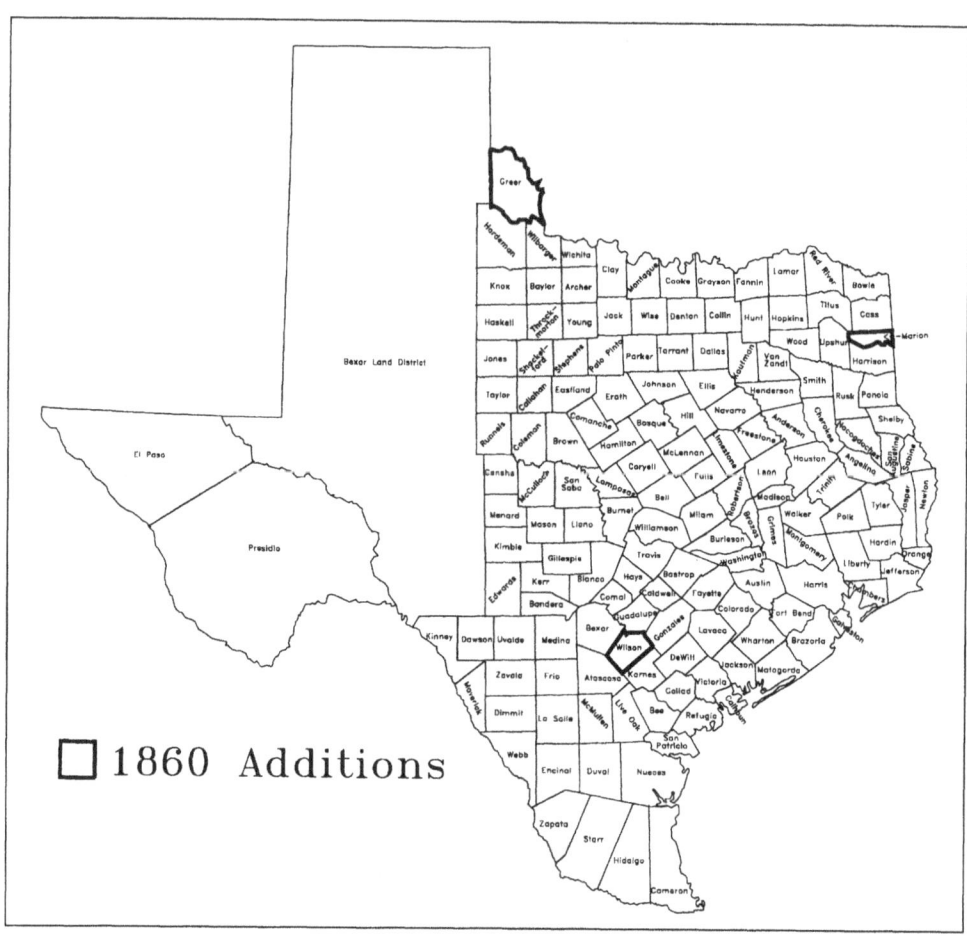

MAP 5-19. Changes in Texas counties, 1860. Map by Luke Gournay.

WILSON COUNTY

Created: From Bexar and Karnes counties on February 13, 1860.
Organized: August, 6, 1860. The first county seat was at Sutherland Springs, where John Irwin's store served as a temporary courthouse. In 1867, the seat of government was moved to Lodi. It was returned to Sutherland Springs in March 1871; then it was moved back to Lodi in July 1871. The last county seat change was to Floresville in 1885.
Boundaries: In 1874, when boundaries underwent a change, the county gained a small amount of land.
Named: For James C. Wilson, who left England for Texas in 1837. Captured in the Mier expedition, he escaped from Mexico and returned to assume public duties under the republic and the state. A legislative act of 1869,

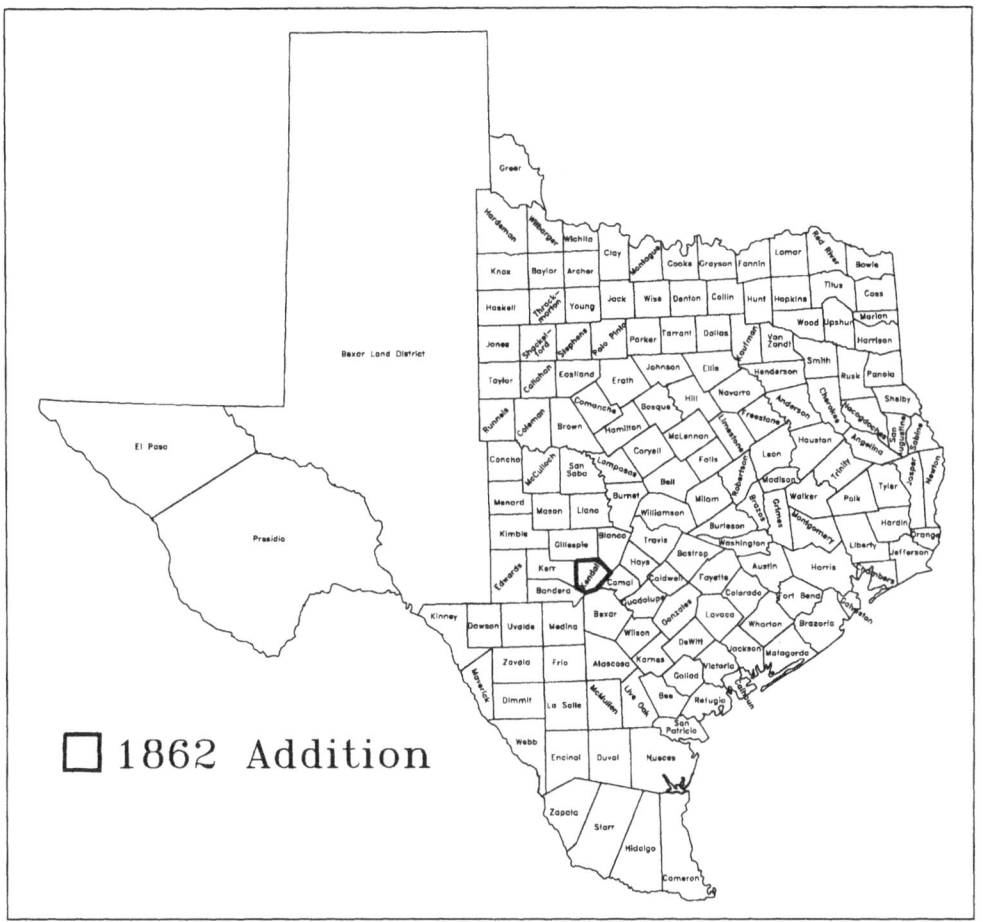

MAP 5-20. Changes in Texas counties, 1862. Map by Luke Gournay.

changing the county name to Cibolo, was ignored. The Wilson name remains in effect today.

1862 Addition: Map 5-20

KENDALL COUNTY

Created: January 10, 1862, out of Blanco and Kerr counties.
Organized: February 18, 1862, when the town of Boerne (formerly Tusculum) was chosen as county seat.
Named: For George Wilkins Kendall, who was born in New Hampshire in 1809. After learning the printing trade under Horace Greeley in New York, he drifted to Boston, North Carolina, and Washington. With a partner, he founded the *New Orleans Picayune* in 1837. From the scene, he reported a

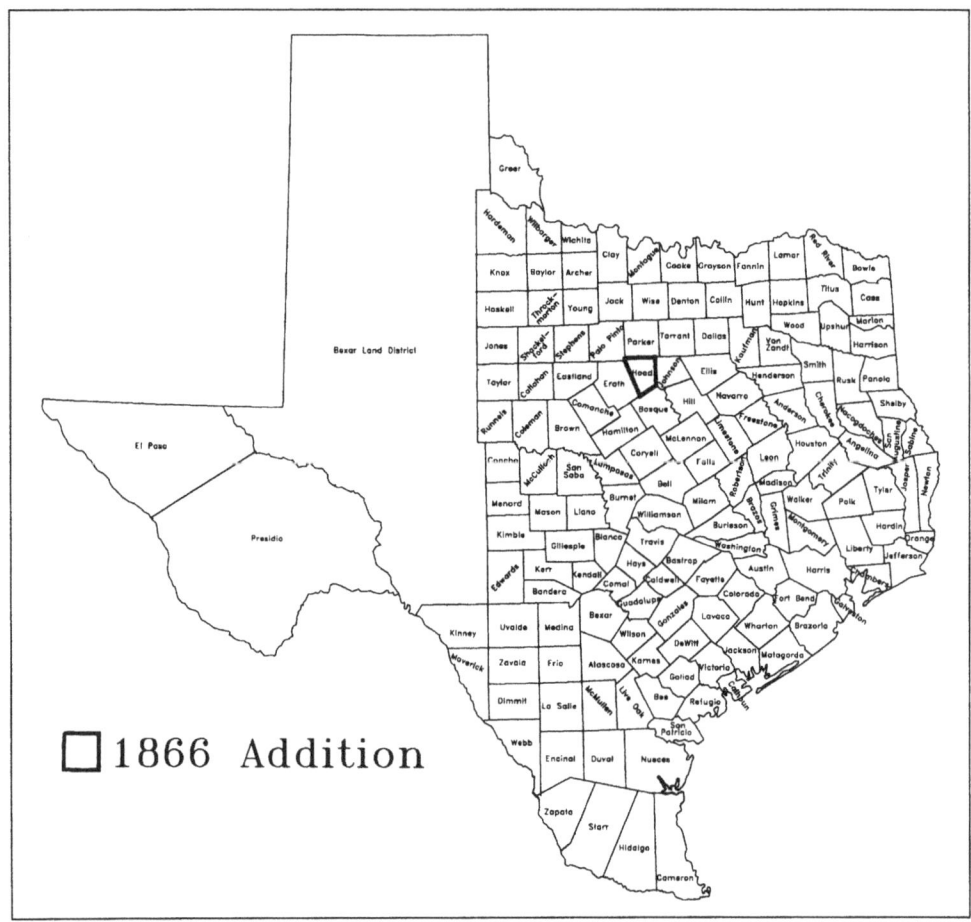

MAP 5-21. Changes in Texas counties, 1866. Map by Luke Gournay.

number of battles and expeditions, with many of his stories going to the *Picayune* by Pony Express. Kendall spent his last days on his ranch in Kendall County.

1866 Activity: Map 5-21

DAWSON COUNTY

This county disappeared from the map in 1866. Its territory and name were removed by legislative acts on September 29 and October 5, 1866.

HOOD COUNTY

Created: November 2, 1866, from Johnson and Erath counties. All or parts of the county at one time or another were in the municipalities of San Felipe de Austin and Viesca.

Organized: December 25, 1866, with Granbury as county seat. Three elections were held before a commission was able to validate the results. An error was made in spelling the name of Gen. Hiram Bronson Granberry, after whom the town was named.

Named: For John Bell Hood, a Kentuckian and West Point graduate who served on the Texas frontier in 1855. At the outbreak of the Civil War, he resigned from the United States Army to join the Confederates. Despite the loss of a leg in the Battle of Gettysburg, Hood fought at Atlanta. At war's end, he settled in New Orleans, where he and his wife died of yellow fever in 1879. Virtually penniless at death, he left nine young orphans behind.

1869 Addition: Map 5-22

SAN JACINTO COUNTY

Created: First in 1869 and again on August 13, 1870, from Liberty, Montgomery, Polk, and Walker counties.

Organized: December 1, 1870, with Cold Spring as county seat. The town, formerly Coonskin, was first renamed Fireman's Hill in 1847, then Cold Spring in 1850. That name was shortened to Coldspring in 1894.

Boundaries: Adjusted in 1874.

Named: For a water hyacinth and a stream. Legend has it that, when missionaries came to this stream in 1760, they found it choked with water hyacinths. The simple name Hyacinth Stream would not suffice; they honored it with the name Saint Hyacinth, or San Jacinto.

1870 Additions: Map 5-23

DELTA COUNTY

Created: August 28, 1868, and recreated July 29, 1870, from parts of Hopkins and Lamar counties.

Organized: October 6, 1870, when Cooper was designated the county seat.

Boundaries: A boundary modification was made in 1871.

Named: Delta because its boundaries are in the shape of the Greek letter *delta*.

RAINS COUNTY

Created: June 9, 1870, from Hunt, Hopkins, and Wood counties.

Organized: December 1, 1870, with Emory picked as county seat.

Named: For Emory Rains, a native Tennessean who came to Texas in 1826. Rains settled in Red River County, then moved to Shelby County, where he represented Shelby and Sabine counties as senator in the Republic of Texas. A delegate to the Constitutional Convention in 1845, he also served as a

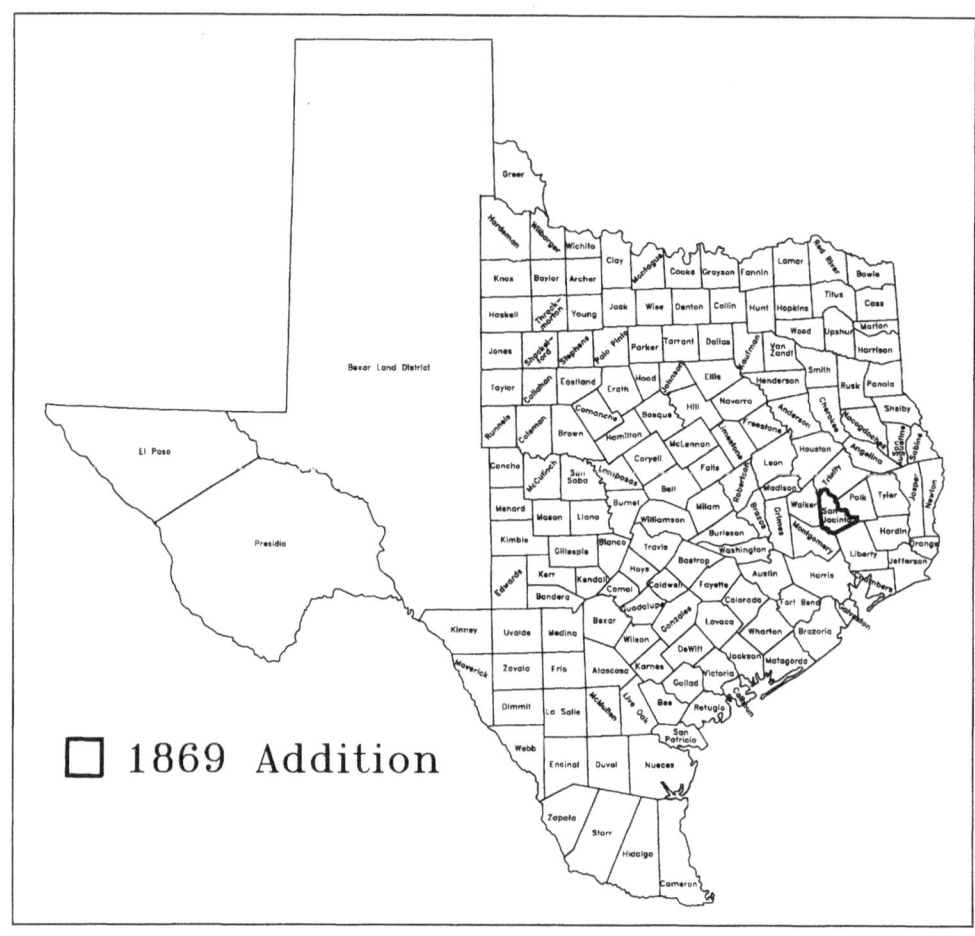

MAP 5-22. Changes in Texas counties, 1869. Map by Luke Gournay.

legislator after annexation. Emory Rains was so well regarded that both county and county seat are named for him.

1871 Additions: Map 5-24

ARANSAS COUNTY

Created: September 18, 1871, from Refugio County.
Organized: 1871. The town of Rockport was the county seat of Refugio County until Aransas County was created and organized. Then Rockport became the Aransas County seat of government, and Refugio became the Refugio county seat.
Named: For the Spanish *Río Nuestra Señora de Aranzazú* (Our Lady of

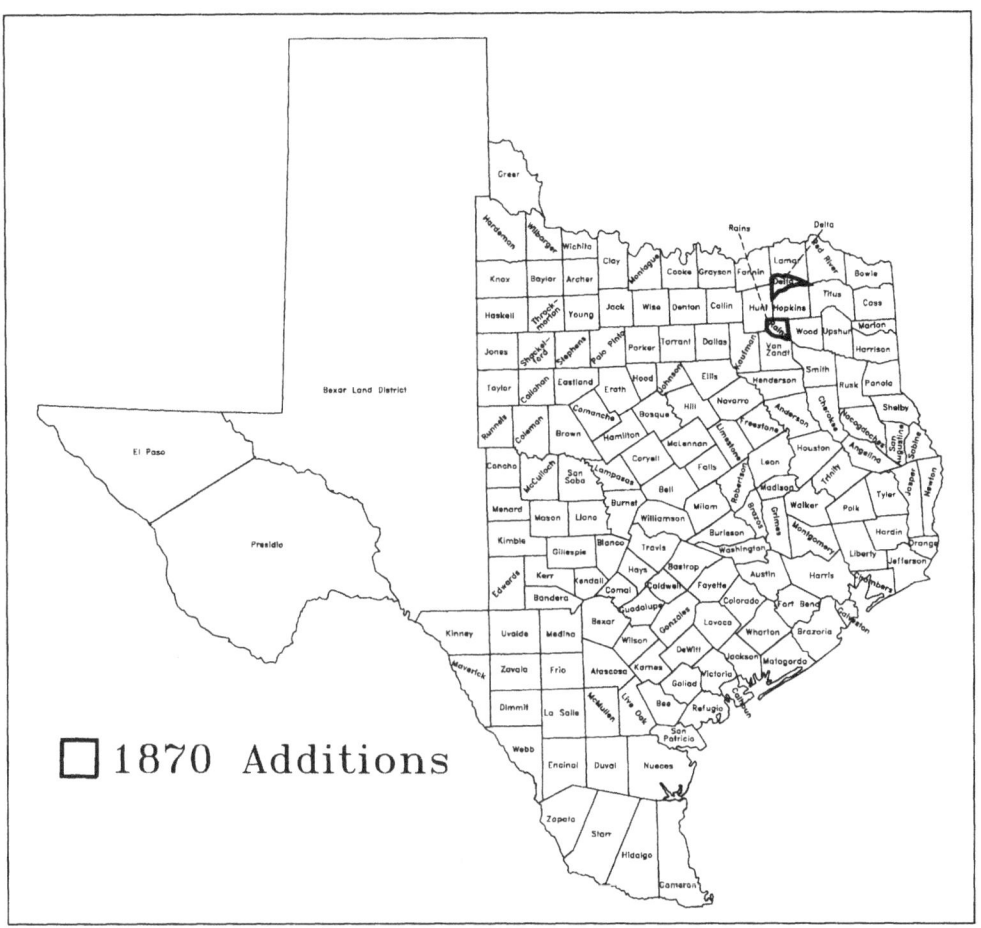

MAP 5-23. Changes in Texas counties, 1870. Map by Luke Gournay.

Aranzazu). Some say the name represents a Spanish saint; other accounts say the name derives from a Spanish palace.

PECOS COUNTY

Created: From Presidio County on May 3, 1871.

Organized: June 13, 1872, with Fort Stockton as the county seat.

Named: For the Pecos River. The geographer and archaeologist Bandelier concluded that the name *Pecos* belongs to the *Qq'ueres* language of New Mexico and is pronounced *Pae-qp*. The name was first mentioned in accounts of a meeting between Juan de Oñate and the Pueblo Indians.

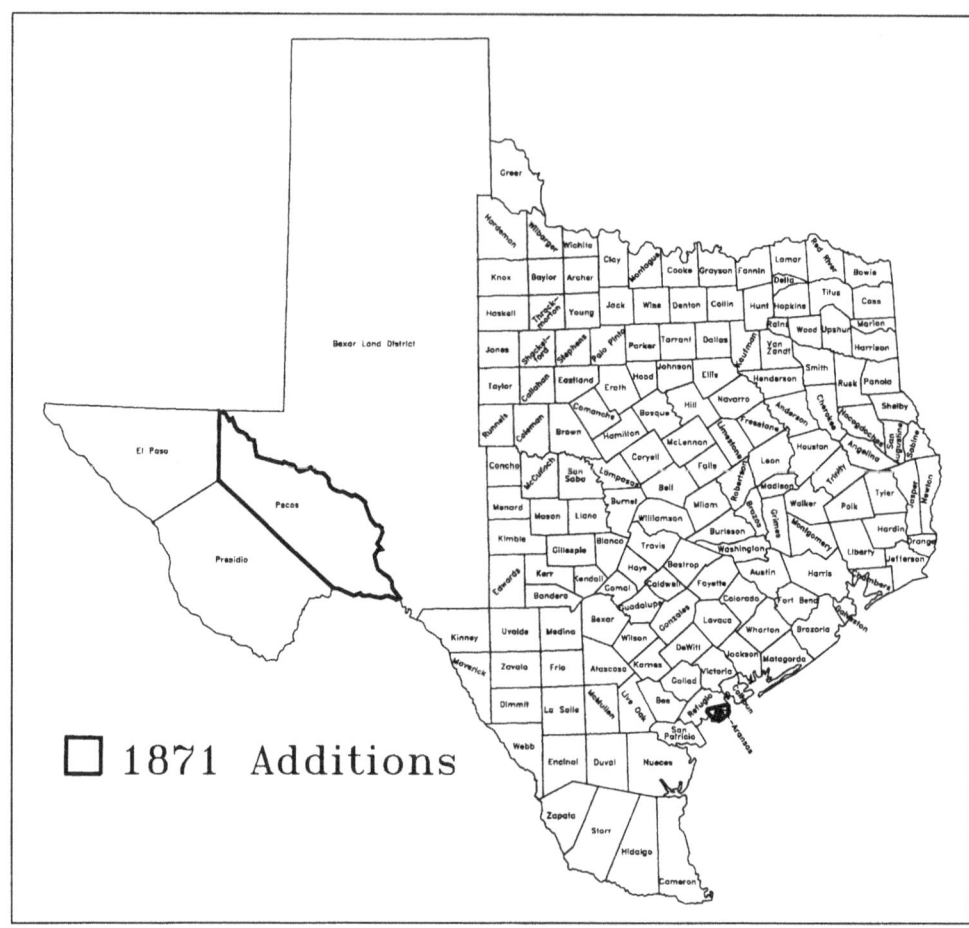

MAP 5-24. Changes in Texas counties, 1871. Map by Luke Gournay.

1873 Additions: Map 5-25

WEGEFARTH COUNTY

Created: From the Bexar Land District on June 2, 1873.

This county was abolished in 1876, when the legislature created fifty-four new Panhandle counties.

GREGG COUNTY

Created: April 12, 1873, out of Rusk County.
Organized: June 28, 1873, with Longview chosen to be the county seat.
Named: For lawyer John Gregg of Alabama, who arrived in Texas in 1852 and was elected district judge in 1861. Gregg donned a uniform during the

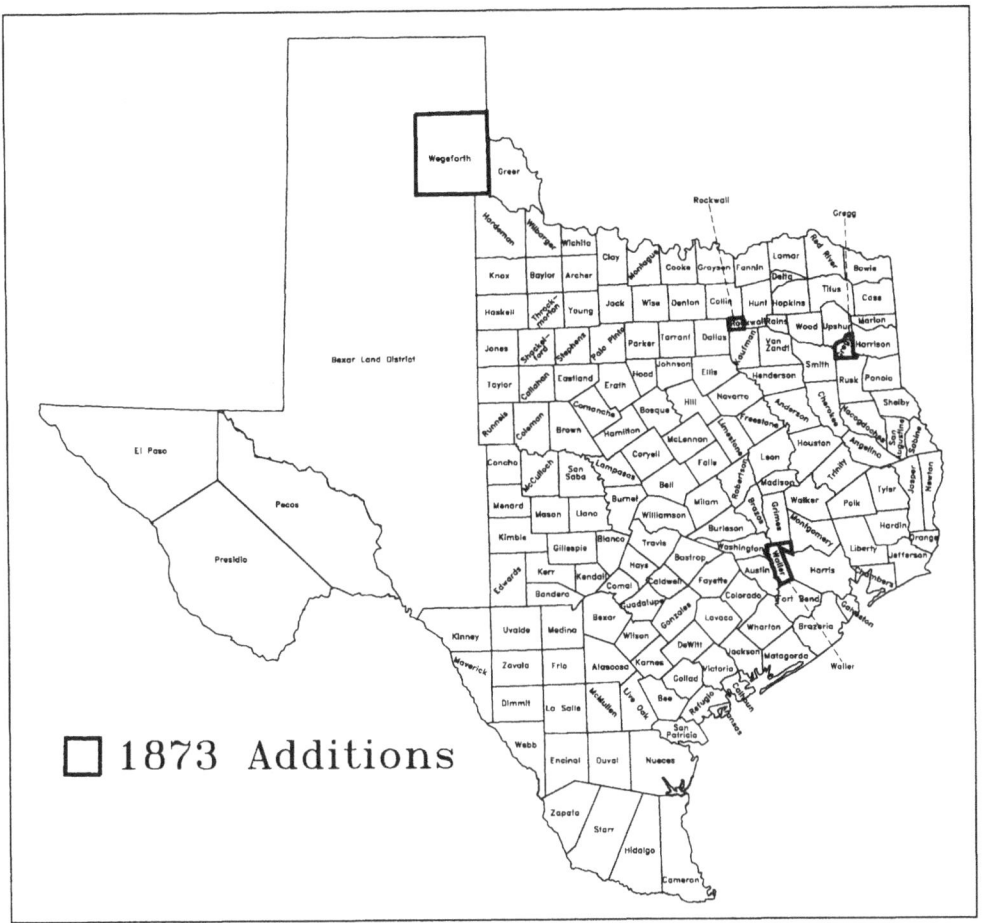

MAP 5-25. Changes in Texas counties, 1873. Map by Luke Gournay.

Civil War, fighting in various battles as a Confederate general. He lost his life while in command of Hood's old brigade in 1864.

ROCKWALL COUNTY

Created: March 1, 1873, from Kaufman County. Rockwall is the smallest county in the state.

Organized: April 23, 1873, with the town of Rockwall as county seat.

Named: For sand dikes which protrude to the surface in many places in the county. Their resemblance to a rock wall gave rise to the county's name. These dikes are natural geological occurrences which appear in many other regions.

WALLER COUNTY

Created: From Austin and Grimes counties on April 28, 1873.
Organized: August 16, 1873, when county officials made Hempstead the seat of government.
Named: For Edwin Waller, a Virginian who came to Texas in 1831. Waller was a member of the Consultation in 1835 and the Convention in 1836. He was a signer of the Texas Declaration of Independence. After helping lay out the city of Austin, Waller became its first mayor in 1840.

1874 Additions: Map 5-26

CAMP COUNTY

Created: Out of Upshur County on April 6, 1874.
Organized: June 20, 1874, with Pittsburg as county seat.
Named: For John La Fayette Camp, a law graduate of the University of Tennessee. He moved to Texas and set up a law practice near Gilmer in 1851. A member of the Constitutional Convention of 1856, Camp was elected state senator in 1874. The county seat, Pittsburg, is named after Maj. W. H. Pitts, who came from Georgia in 1850.

LEE COUNTY

Created: From parts of Bastrop, Fayette, Washington, and Burleson counties, on April 14, 1874.
Organized: June 2, 1874, when Giddings was picked as county seat. The original settlers were Wends, who came from Germany in 1854, founding the town of Serbin.
Named: For Confederate Gen. Robert E. Lee.

TOM GREEN COUNTY

Created: March 13, 1874, taking 12,500 square miles from the Bexar Land District. In the years afterward, twelve other counties were formed out of Tom Green, leaving it with an area of 1,503 square miles.
Organized: January 5, 1875. Ben Ficklin, a station on the Butterfield Overland Mail Route, won over the town of Saint Angela to become county seat. After a flash flood destroyed Ben Ficklin in 1882, San Angelo became the center of county government.
Named: For Gen. Thomas Green, a native Virginian who arrived in Texas in time to fight at San Jacinto. After Texas' independence, he served as Fayette County surveyor and clerk of the republic's supreme court. Green also was busy joining one expedition after another, when, in 1864, he was killed at the Battle of Blair's Landing on Louisiana's Red River.

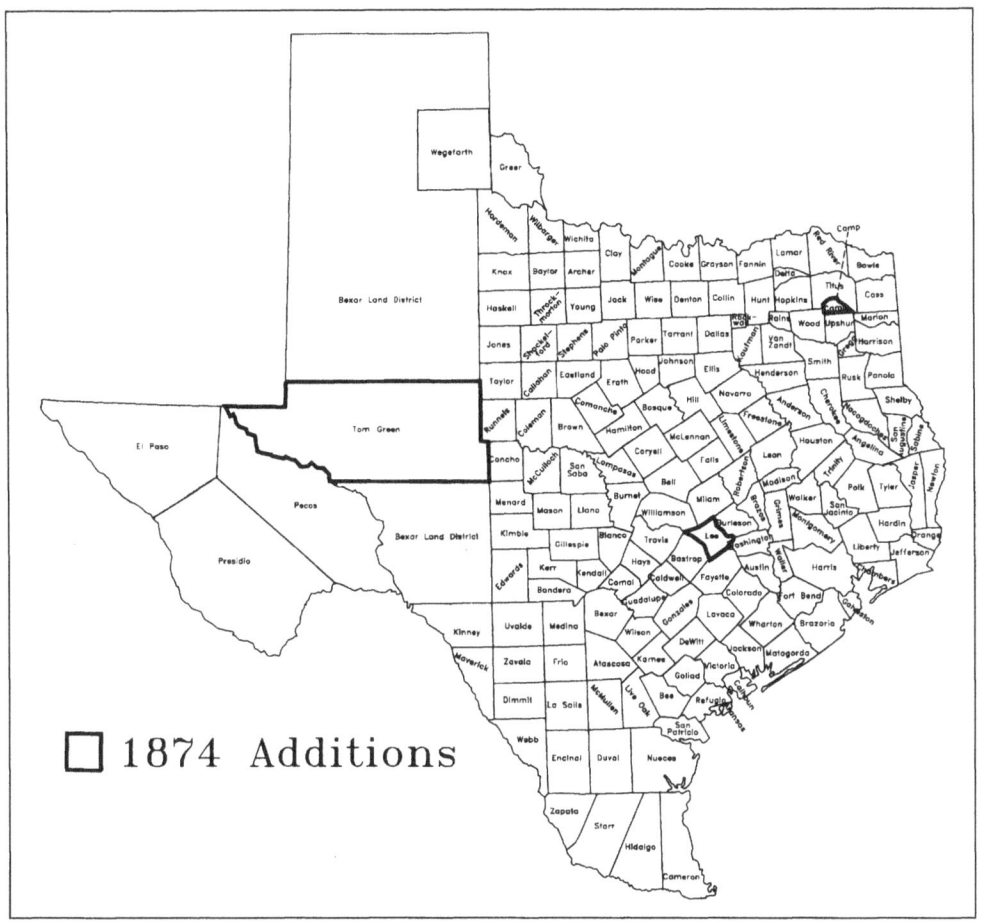

MAP 5-26. Changes in Texas counties, 1874. Map by Luke Gournay.

1875 Additions: Map 5-27

CROCKETT COUNTY

Created: January 22, 1875, out of the Bexar Land District.
Organized: July 14, 1891, when Ozona was selected as county seat.
Named: For David Crockett, the famous Tennessean. Crockett was elected to the United States Congress in 1827, 1829, and 1831, but his defeat in a fourth race left him disgusted with politics. Saying farewell to his family, Crockett came to Texas, where he went directly into war. He joined forces with Travis at the Alamo and, on March 6, 1836, gave his life with the other heroes.

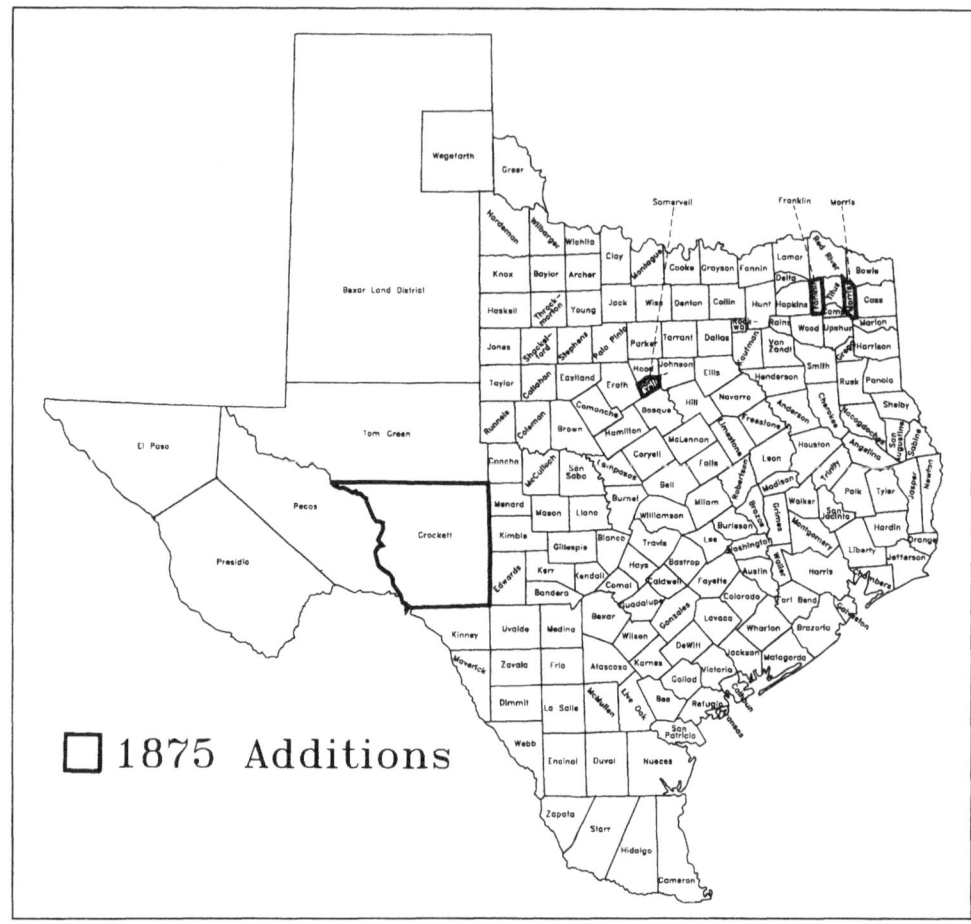

MAP 5-27. Changes in Texas counties, 1875. Map by Luke Gournay.

FRANKLIN COUNTY

Created: From Titus County on March 6, 1875.

Organized: April 30, 1875, when the county seat was placed at Mount Vernon.

Named: For Judge Benjamin C. Franklin, who came to Texas from Georgia in 1835. Soon after his arrival, he entered the war for independence, fighting in campaigns from Gonzales to San Jacinto. After the war, Franklin served as district judge and state legislator.

MORRIS COUNTY

Created: From Titus County on May 11, 1846.

Organized: July 13, 1846, with Daingerfield as the county seat.

Named: Either for Richard Morris of Virginia or W. W. Morris of North

Carolina, both of whom migrated to Texas. Richard Morris came to Galveston in 1838, where Texas President Lamar appointed him district judge in 1841. W. W. Morris served in the Texas Legislature.

SOMERVELL COUNTY

Created: From parts of Hood and Johnson counties on March 13, 1875, with the county's name misspelled in the legislative act. To correct the error, the legislature amended the act on August 15, 1876.
Organized: 1875, when Glen Rose became the county seat.
Named: For General Alexander Somervell, best known for his leadership of the Somervell expedition. This was a punitive expedition against Mexico, undertaken in 1842 in retaliation for Mexican raids into Texas. The attempted reprisals were politically motivated and did not succeed. They led only to the ill-fated Mier expedition of 1842.

1876 Additions: Map 5-28

In 1876 the legislature took a giant step in the creation of counties. Covering the entire Panhandle and the Llano Estacado, the state created fifty-four new counties.

These were: Andrews, Armstrong, Bailey, Borden, Briscoe, Carson, Castro, Childress, Cochran, Collingsworth, Cottle, Crosby, Dallam, Dawson, Deaf Smith, Dickens, Donley, Fisher, Floyd, Gaines, Garza, Gray, Hale, Hall, Hansford, Hartley, Hemphill, Hockley, Howard, Hutchinson, Kent, King, Lamb, Lipscomb, Lubbock, Lynn, Martin, Mitchell, Moore, Motley, Nolan, Ochiltree, Oldham, Parmer, Potter, Randall, Roberts, Scurry, Sherman, Stonewall, Swisher, Terry, Wheeler, and Yoakum.

The legislature generated these counties in one fell swoop, as a measure of legal economy. It was clear that, while most did not have sufficient population to be organized immediately, in the not-too-distant future they would grow to the requisite size. Having given rail companies free land in exchange for the construction of railroads, the legislators anticipated that the rail lines would bring new settlers to these western areas. And so it happened.

A brief narrative for each new county follows.

ANDREWS COUNTY

Andrews County was attached successively to several counties for judicial purposes: Shackelford County in 1876, the Howard Land District in 1882, the Martin Land District in 1887, and Martin County in 1891. The county was organized in 1910, with the town of Andrews as county seat. It was

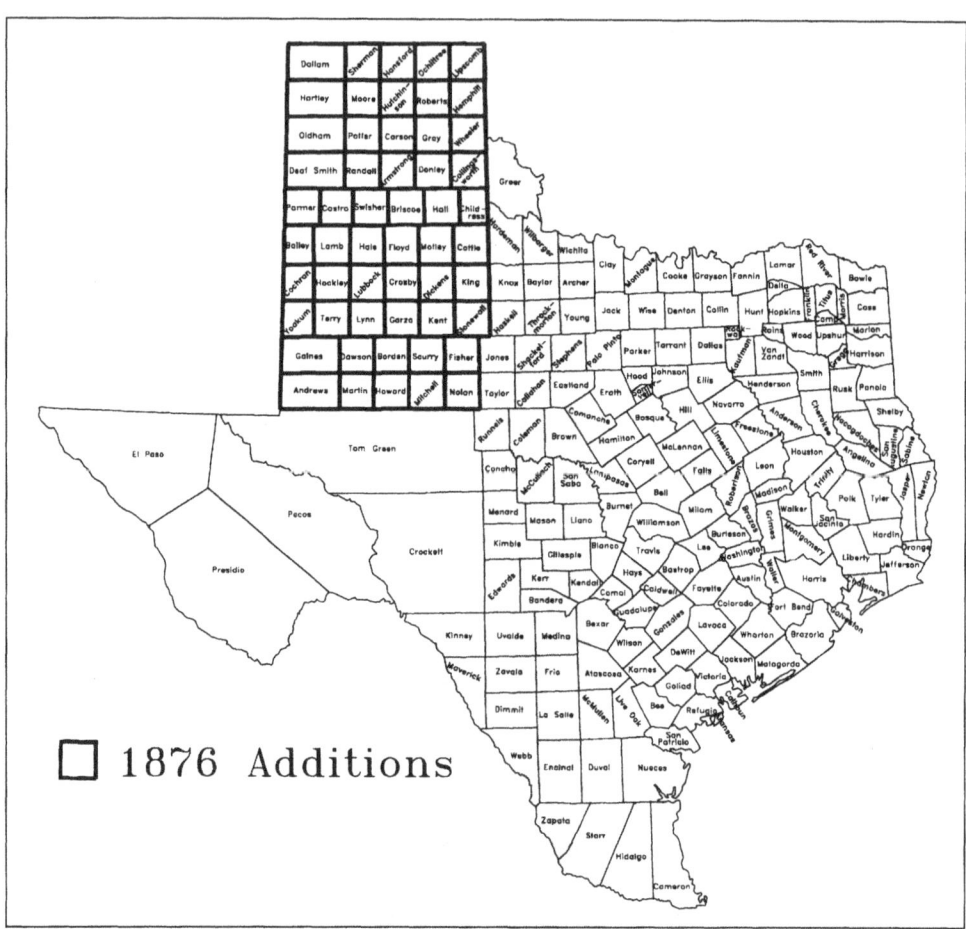

MAP 5-28. Changes in Texas counties, 1876. Map by Luke Gournay.

named for Richard Andrews who joined in the Texas Revolution and was wounded in the battle of Gonzales on October 2, 1835. Shortly thereafter, on October 28, while with Stephen F. Austin, James Bowie, and James W. Fannin at the battle of Concepción, he was killed.

ARMSTRONG COUNTY

Armstrong County was organized on March 8, 1890, with Claude as the county seat. Completion of the Fort Worth and Denver Railroad in 1887 provided the population boost necessary for organization. The county was named for "The Armstrong family" with no clues in the act creating the county as to which Armstrong family was meant. There were six prominent Armstrong families at the time.

BAILEY COUNTY

Bailey County was not organized until 1917, when Muleshoe became the county seat. The county's namesake was Peter J. Bailey, who died at the Alamo.

BORDEN COUNTY

Borden County was named for Gail Borden, Jr., a prolific inventor widely known for developing a process for condensing milk. A petition for organization was approved in 1890. Gail, the only town in the county, was chosen as county seat on March 17, 1891.

BRISCOE COUNTY

Briscoe County, named for Andrew Briscoe, a compatriot of Ben Milam in the siege of Bexar, was organized on January 11, 1892. Silverton was chosen as county seat. Extension of the Fort Worth and Denver Railroad to this area was a major factor in the county's development.

CARSON COUNTY

Carson County was named for Samuel Price Carson, secretary of state of the Republic of Texas under President Burnet. It was organized on June 26, 1888, with Panhandle (formerly Panhandle City) named as county seat. Two railroads—the Fort Worth and Denver, and the Rock Island and Gulf—helped to populate the county in the late 1800s.

CASTRO COUNTY

Castro County became organized in 1891, and Dimmitt was designated as the county seat. The county was named after Henri Castro, an empresario in the Republic of Texas.

CHILDRESS COUNTY

Childress County, named for George C. Childress, author of the Texas Declaration of Independence, was attached first to Clay and then to Donley County for judicial purposes. Childress County was organized on April 11, 1887, with the town of Childress as county seat.

COCHRAN COUNTY

Cochran County delayed its organization until 1924, first because of hostile Indians and later because of its remote location. At the time of organization, Morton was selected as county seat. The county initially was attached to Hockley and Lubbock counties for its judicial needs. Cochran County was named for Robert Cochran, who died at the Alamo.

COLLINGSWORTH COUNTY

Collingsworth County was named after James Collinsworth, who was a leader in establishing the Republic of Texas. In an error that was never corrected, the legislature misspelled his name. Prior to organization, the county was administered by Wheeler and Childress counties.

Although Pearl was the leading candidate for county seat, cowboys working at the Rocking Chair Ranch, who were English, wanted Wellington. They brought out the vote and won on September 30, 1890.

COTTLE COUNTY

Cottle County was named after George Washington Cottle, who died at the Alamo. Unsettled for sixteen years, the county was attached to Childress County before being organized in January 1892. Paducah was chosen as county seat.

CROSBY COUNTY

Crosby County was organized on September 11, 1886, with Estacado as the county seat. Emma took that honor in 1891 but was replaced by Crosbyton in 1912, when the Crosbyton and South Plains Railroad was completed from Lubbock to Crosbyton. The county was named for Stephen Crosby, who served as chief clerk in the Texas Land Office from 1845 to 1867.

DALLAM COUNTY

Dallam County was organized on September 8, 1891, after the Fort Worth and Denver City Railroad reached Texline, the first county seat. The county government was moved to Dalhart in 1893. The county was named for James Wilmer Dallam, a publisher of legal digests.

DAWSON COUNTY

Dawson County was named for Nicholas Mosby Dawson, who fought at San Jacinto and later was massacred at the Battle of Salado. Initially attached to Howard County, the county became organized on February 13, 1905, as Lamesa and Chicago vied to become the county seat. Soon after Lamesa won, the two towns consolidated.

DEAF SMITH COUNTY

Deaf Smith County was named after Erastus "Deaf" Smith, popular activist and participant in the Texas Revolution. It was organized on December 1, 1890, with Hereford selected as county seat.

DICKENS COUNTY

Dickens County took its name from J. Dickens, who died at the Alamo. A town of the same name became the county seat upon organization on March 14, 1891.

DONLEY COUNTY

Donley County was organized on March 22, 1882, with Clarendon as county seat. The county was named for a prominent East Texas lawyer, Stockton P. Donley.

FISHER COUNTY

Fisher County lay dormant until railroad construction began in 1881. Organized on April 27, 1886, with Roby as county seat, the county was named for Samuel Rhoads Fisher, a signer of the Texas Declaration of Independence. Fisher was appointed and then fired as secretary of the navy, by Republic of Texas President Sam Houston.

FLOYD COUNTY

Floyd County was organized on May 28, 1890, but a bitter struggle for county seat ensued. Contestants were Della Plain, Lockney, and Floyd City. Floyd City was chosen, but the election was contested from the district court to the Texas Supreme Court, where Floyd City prevailed. Since its name coincided with that of another city in Texas, it was changed to Floydada that year. The "Ada" was added in recognition of Mrs. Ada Price, a pioneer in the area.

GAINES COUNTY

Gaines County was named by West Texas settlers for James Gaines, alcalde of the Municipality of Sabine in 1823. Active in civic affairs, Gaines helped to draft and then signed the Texas Declaration of Independence. Seminole became county seat when the county was organized twenty-nine years after its creation, on October 24, 1905.

GARZA COUNTY

Garza County took its name from that of a pioneer family. It was organized on June 15, 1907, after Charles William Post founded Post City, a planned model townsite. This townsite had to be moved a few miles to place it near the center of the county. The town was named after Post, the originator of Postum and Post Toasties.

GRAY COUNTY

Gray County recognized Peter W. Gray, a Texas lawyer, legislator, and judge. Gray County finally had enough voters to become organized on May 27, 1902, with Lefors chosen as county seat. Large accumulations of oil and gas, discovered in the middle 1920s, made Pampa a center of activity, and in 1928 Pampa became the county seat.

HALE COUNTY

Hale County, located at the center of the Llano Estacado, was attached for judicial purposes to Baylor, Donley, and Crosby counties successively. Organization came on August 4, 1888, with Plainview named county seat. The county name honors Lt. John C. Hale, who died at San Jacinto.

HALL COUNTY

Hall County was organized on June 23, 1890, with Memphis as county seat. The county was named for Warren D. C. Hall, a North Carolinian who settled in Texas in 1835. Hall was adjutant general of the Republic of Texas under President Burnet.

HANSFORD COUNTY

Hansford County, named for the political leader and judge John M. Hansford, was known by early explorers as the "Great American Desert." At organization on March 11, 1889, Farwell and Hansford vied to become the county seat but Hansford won. When the North Texas and Santa Fe Railroad reached Spearman in 1920, that town became the hub of business activity and replaced Hansford as county seat.

HARTLEY COUNTY

Named after Oliver Cromwell Hartley, a Virginia lawyer who settled at Galveston, Hartley County was organized on February 9, 1891. The town of Hartley became the county seat and remained such until 1903. In November 1896 and again in May 1903, elections were held to move the county government to Channing. After Channing won the second election, the wooden courthouse was rolled to the new site by cowboys from the XIT Ranch.

HEMPHILL COUNTY

Eleven years after its creation, Hemphill County saw the arrival of the Southern Kansas Railroad, and that line provided the stimulus for settlement. Organization came on July 5, 1887, when Canadian became the county seat. The county was named for Judge John Hemphill, a South Carolinian who came to Texas in 1838 and assumed important judicial positions.

Hockley County was belatedly organized in February 1921, forty-six years after its creation. The contestants for county seat were Ropesville and a vacant plot called Hockley City. After Hockley City won the election, it changed its name to Levelland. This county was named for George W. Hockley, who came from Philadelphia. He commanded the artillery at San Jacinto, then served as secretary of war in the Republic of Texas under President Sam Houston.

HOWARD COUNTY

Howard County was attached to Mitchell County for legal matters until its organization on June 15, 1882. At that time the principal town, Big Spring, became county seat. The county was named for Volney Erskine Howard, who came from Maine, worked on newspapers in the South, and arrived at San Antonio in 1844. Howard was a state senator and then a United States congressman.

HUTCHINSON COUNTY

Hutchinson County was organized in 1901, with the county seat established at Stinnett. The county was named for attorney Anderson Hutchinson, a Virginian who came to Texas in 1841. Hutchinson became a district judge in San Antonio.

KENT COUNTY

Kent County was attached to Scurry County until it could support a local government. Organized on November 8, 1892, with the county seat placed at Clairemont, Kent County took its name from Andrew Kent. Having come to Texas in 1828, Kent, with thirty-two others from Gonzales, went to Travis' aid at the Alamo, where he died.

KING COUNTY

King County finally reached the population required for organization in 1891. In a contest between Guthrie and Ashville for the county seat designation, Guthrie won; it has retained that position. William P. King, for whom the county was named, joined Andrew Kent and others in responding to Travis' call. He perished at the Alamo.

LAMB COUNTY

Lamb County was organized on June 20, 1908, when Olton was named the county seat. In 1929, 1932, and 1937, Littlefield called elections in attempts to become the county seat. Finally, a 1946 election was successful in forcing this change. The county was named after Lt. George A. Lamb, who died at the Battle of San Jacinto.

LIPSCOMB COUNTY

Lipscomb County was reached by the Panhandle and Santa Fe Railroad in 1880. Cheap land attracted enough settlers to organize the county on June 6, 1887, with a government center at the town of Lipscomb. The county is named for Abner S. Lipscomb, a South Carolinian who studied law under John C. Calhoun. Coming to Texas in 1839, he served in the cabinet of President Lamar of the Republic of Texas and then became a judge in the Texas Supreme Court.

LUBBOCK COUNTY

Lubbock County was organized March 10, 1891, with the town of Lubbock as county seat. The name commemorated Thomas S. Lubbock, who saw action with Ben Milam in the siege of Bexar. Lubbock later joined the Texas Santa Fe expedition but was captured and imprisoned in Mexico. After escaping, he returned to Texas to join the Somervell expedition. Fortunately, Lubbock left the expedition before it met its fate as the Mier affair.

LYNN COUNTY

Lynn County was organized in 1903, twenty-seven years after its creation; Tahoka was chosen as the county seat. The county is named for W. Lynn (or Linn), who died in the Alamo. Little is known of Lynn's life before the Alamo.

MARTIN COUNTY

Martin County was attached to Howard County for judicial purposes until it was organized on November 14, 1884, with Mariensfield (formerly Grelton) chosen as county seat. Mariensfield voters changed its name to Stanton in 1889. The county was named after Wylie Martin, an alcalde in Austin's colony. Active in the Texas Revolution, Martin later served in the Texas Senate.

MITCHELL COUNTY

Mitchell County, originally part of the John Cameron Grant, was organized on January 10, 1881, with Colorado City named as county seat. Coming in 1881, the Texas and Pacific Railroad provided the stimulus for settlement.

The county was named for the brothers Asa and Eli Mitchell, who came to Texas in the 1820s. They played active leadership roles in the development of the Republic of Texas.

Moore County was organized July 6, 1892, and Dumas became the county seat. The county was named for Commodore Edwin Ward Moore, who was appointed captain of the navy by Republic of Texas President Sam Houston. A disagreement between the two caused Moore to resign his commission and position. The president of the North Plains and Santa Fe Railroad named the town of Dumas for himself.

MOTLEY COUNTY

Motley County was organized on February 25, 1891, with Matador as county seat. The majority of the voters were cowboys of the Matador Ranch. Named after Dr. Junius William Mottley, the county name was misspelled at the time of organization. A graduate in medicine at Transylvania University, Dr. Mottley moved to Gonzales, Texas, in 1835. Fighting with the revolutionary forces, he died in the Battle of San Jacinto.

NOLAN COUNTY

Nolan County voters chose the Sweetwater Post Office as temporary seat of government for Nolan County, on January 10, 1881. On March 31, 1881, an election fixed Sweetwater, two miles away, as the permanent county seat.

The county was named for Philip Nolan. A horsetrader, Nolan was commissioned by Baron de Carondelet, governor of Louisiana, to obtain horses for Louisiana regiments. His activities aroused the suspicions of Spanish officials, who set a trap and killed him.

OCHILTREE COUNTY

Ochiltree County was organized on February 21, 1889, when the town of Ochiltree became the county seat. After the North Texas and Santa Fe Railroad was built in 1919, Perryton, established on the rail line, became the county seat.

The county was named for William Beck Ochiltree, who came to Nacogdoches in 1839. He was appointed district judge of the Fifth Judicial District of the Republic of Texas in 1842, and secretary of treasury of the republic in 1844. Ochiltree was the last person to hold the office of attorney general of the Republic of Texas.

OLDHAM COUNTY

Oldham County was organized on June 12, 1881, with Tascosa named as county seat. The judicial district created in Tascosa in 1881 served sixteen nearby unorganized counties. After the Chicago, Rock Island and Gulf Railroad was built, Vega outgrew Tascosa and replaced it as the county seat in 1915.

Williamson S. Oldham, for whom the county was named, came to Texas from Tennessee in 1849. A publisher of legal digests, Oldham served in the Confederate government.

Parmer County was attached to Oldham County until it could organize as a governmental entity in 1907, with Farwell as the county seat. This county was named for Martin Parmer, from Virginia. Moving to East Texas in 1825, he helped foment the Fredonian Rebellion. After signing the Texas Declaration of Independence, Parmer was elected to numerous civil posts. His family line was not kept intact because of a misspelling: his children all carried the name of Palmer.

Potter County was organized on September 6, 1887, with Ragtown as county seat. Ragtown started out as a shantytown but was relocated to a new site laid out by Henry B. Sanborn in 1889. It was renamed Oneida and then Amarillo.

The county was named for another colorful Texas figure, Robert Potter. A signer of the Texas Declaration of Independence, Potter became secretary of the Texas Navy. Leaving a turbulent legacy described in several books, he was assassinated at his home by one of his enemies on March 2, 1842, at the age of forty-two.

Randall County elected officers and chose a county seat, Canyon City, on July 27, 1889. That town's name was later changed to Canyon. From the time of creation until organization, the county was judicially served in succession by Wheeler, Oldham, Donley, and Potter counties.

The county was named for Gen. Horace Randall, a Tennessean and West Point graduate, who served in the United States cavalry on the Texas frontiers until the Civil War began. As a brigadier general in the Confederate forces, Randall was killed at Jenkins' Ferry in 1864.

Roberts County was attached to Wheeler County until organized on January 10, 1889. During a dispute over placement of the county seat, citizens of the town of Miami took over the government base and elected county officials. Canadian River residents seized the records, built a courthouse, and moved the government to Parnell. In an 1898 election, the argument was settled by ballot, with Miami resuming its position as county seat.

The residents named their county after two distinguished Virginians who came to Texas: John S. Roberts and Oran Milo Roberts. Politically inclined, they served in various important positions in the Republic of Texas.

SCURRY COUNTY

Scurry County received its first settlers when they arrived at a trading post at the present site of the town of Snyder. The post became a townsite and, when the county was organized in 1884, a county seat.

The county was named for William Redi Scurry, a Tennessee attorney who came to Texas in 1840. While a member of the Confederate forces, Scurry was killed in the Civil War.

SHERMAN COUNTY

Sherman County was not organized until June 13, 1889. The first courthouse was built in 1891 at Coldwater, the county seat. After the railroad was constructed in 1900, Stratford prospered and took over as seat of government. When Coldwater residents protested with threats to retake the county records by force, they were restrained by armed guards. Stratford won the standoff and retained the county courts.

The county was named after Gen. Sidney Sherman, who left a business in Kentucky to lead a company of volunteers in the fight at San Jacinto.

STONEWALL COUNTY

Stonewall County was attached to Jones County until organized in 1888. Rayner, a cattle camp on the Rayner Ranch, was selected as county seat. Two years later, Aspermont launched a campaign to become the center of government. Aspermont won in an election, but the argument continued until 1898, when the courts finally settled the issue in favor of Aspermont.

The county was named for Gen. Thomas Jonathan "Stonewall" Jackson.

SWISHER COUNTY

Swisher County was organized on July 17, 1890, when Tulia, with a misspelled name, became the county seat. The name was meant to be Tullie, after nearby Tule Creek.

The county was named for John G. Swisher, a Tennessean who migrated to Robertson's Colony in 1833. He joined Ben Milam at Bexar and then helped to establish the new government.

TERRY COUNTY

Terry County, organized on July 5, 1904, was the scene of competition between the towns of Gomez and Brownfield for the courthouse and its officialdom. By three votes, Brownfield won the election and so became the county seat.

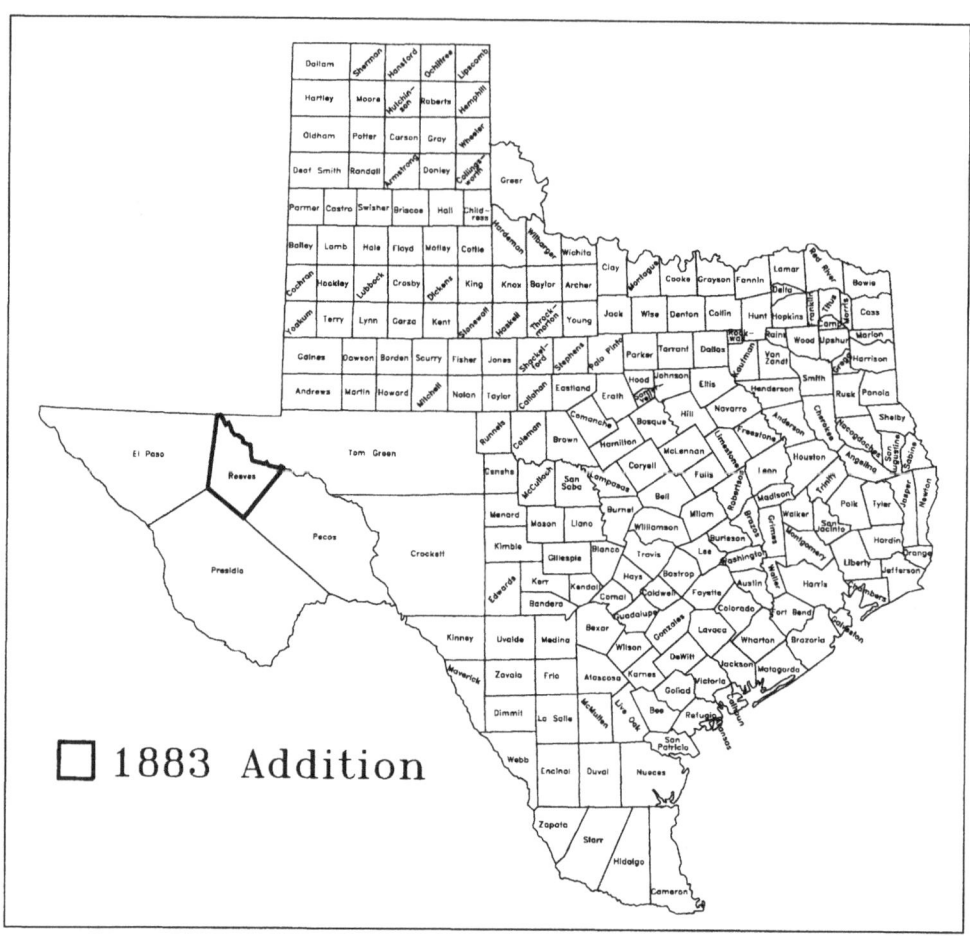

MAP 5-29. Changes in Texas counties, 1883. Map by Luke Gournay.

Terry County took its name from Benjamin Franklin Terry, who came from Kentucky to Brazoria County, Texas, in 1831. Too young to go to San Jacinto, he led a regiment known as "Terry's Texas Rangers" in the Civil War.

WHEELER COUNTY

Wheeler County, by April 12, 1879, had a population sufficient for organization. After Sweetwater was made the county seat, its name was changed to Mobeetie, the Indian word for Sweetwater. Since Wheeler was the first Panhandle county to organize, fourteen other counties were attached to it for judicial attention. In the late 1800s, a storm demolished Mobeetie, causing the county seat to move to Wheeler in 1906.

The county was named for Royal T. Wheeler, who came from Vermont in 1838. Wheeler took part in affairs for the Republic of Texas and the State of Texas.

YOAKUM COUNTY

Yoakum County was named for Henderson Yoakum, a Tennessee lawyer who came to Texas in 1845 to practice law and write history. He settled in the Huntsville area and spent most of his life in East Texas.

The county was organized in 1907, with Plains as county seat, after Texas placed land on the market at prices meant to entice settlers.

1883 Addition: Map 5-29

REEVES COUNTY

Created: From Pecos County on April 14, 1883.
Organized: November 4, 1884, when Pecos City was chosen as county seat. Initially established as a rail station called Pecos Station, the name was later shortened to Pecos.
Named: For George R. Reeves, a Tennessean who migrated into Texas in 1845, to venture into farming and cattle raising. He held positions of sheriff, tax collector, and legislator before the Civil War began. In the Eleventh Texas Cavalry, he served at locations east of the Mississippi. After the war, he returned to the Texas Legislature, where he was speaker of the House of Representatives.

1885 Additions: Map 5-30

MIDLAND COUNTY

Created: March 4, 1885, out of Tom Green County.
Organized: June 15, 1885, with Midland as county seat.
Named: For its location midway between Fort Worth and El Paso on the Texas and Pacific rail line.

VAL VERDE COUNTY

Created: March 24, 1885, from portions of three counties: Kinney, Crockett, and Pecos.
Organized: May 2, 1885, when Del Rio became the county seat.
Named: To commemorate the battle fought at Val Verde, New Mexico, on February 19, 1862. In this encounter, the Sibley expedition attempted to bring New Mexico under Confederate control. Led by Gen. Tom Green, the Confederate troops won at Val Verde but were forced into retreat at Glorieta.

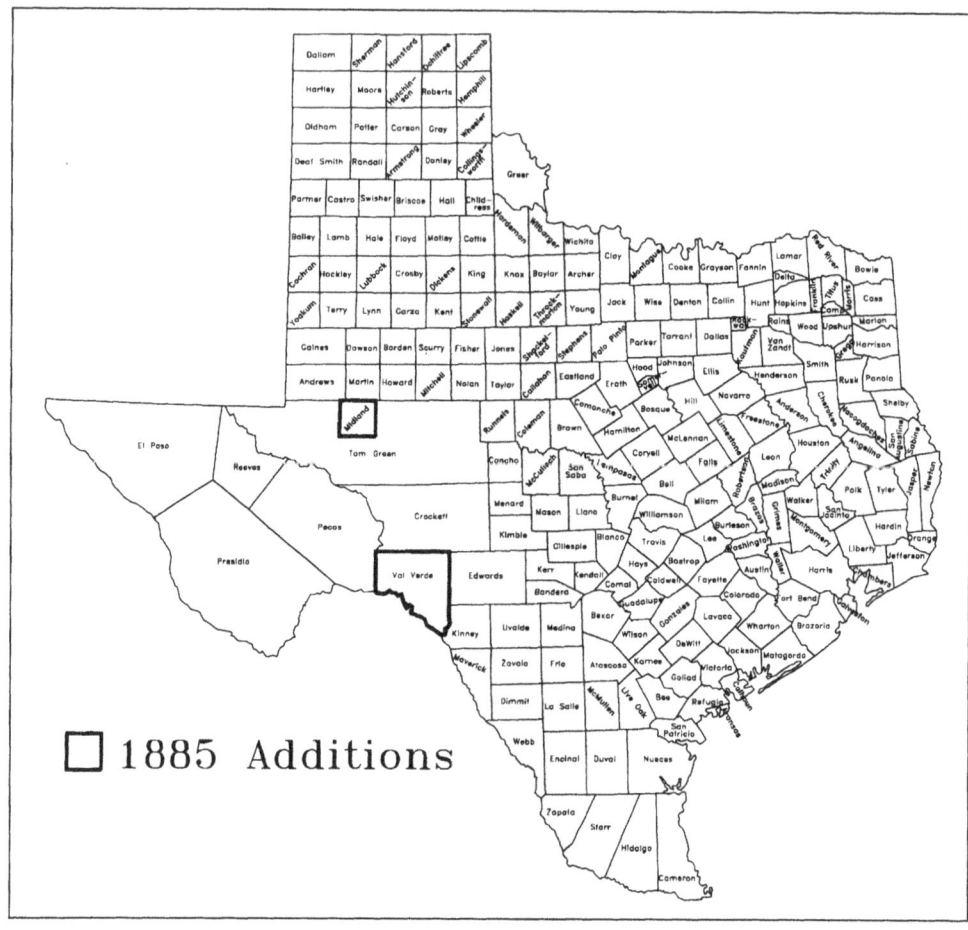

MAP 5-30. Changes in Texas counties, 1885. Map by Luke Gournay.

1887 Additions: Map 5-31

BUCHEL AND FOLEY COUNTIES

Created: March 15, 1887. They were taken from Presidio County, but were never organized. Both were abolished in April 1897.

BREWSTER COUNTY

Created: Out of Presidio County on February 2, 1887.
Organized: February 26, 1887, with Murpheyville (formerly Osborne) made the county seat. In the same year, Murpheyville's name was changed to Alpine.
Boundaries: In 1897, when the counties of Buchel and Foley were abol-

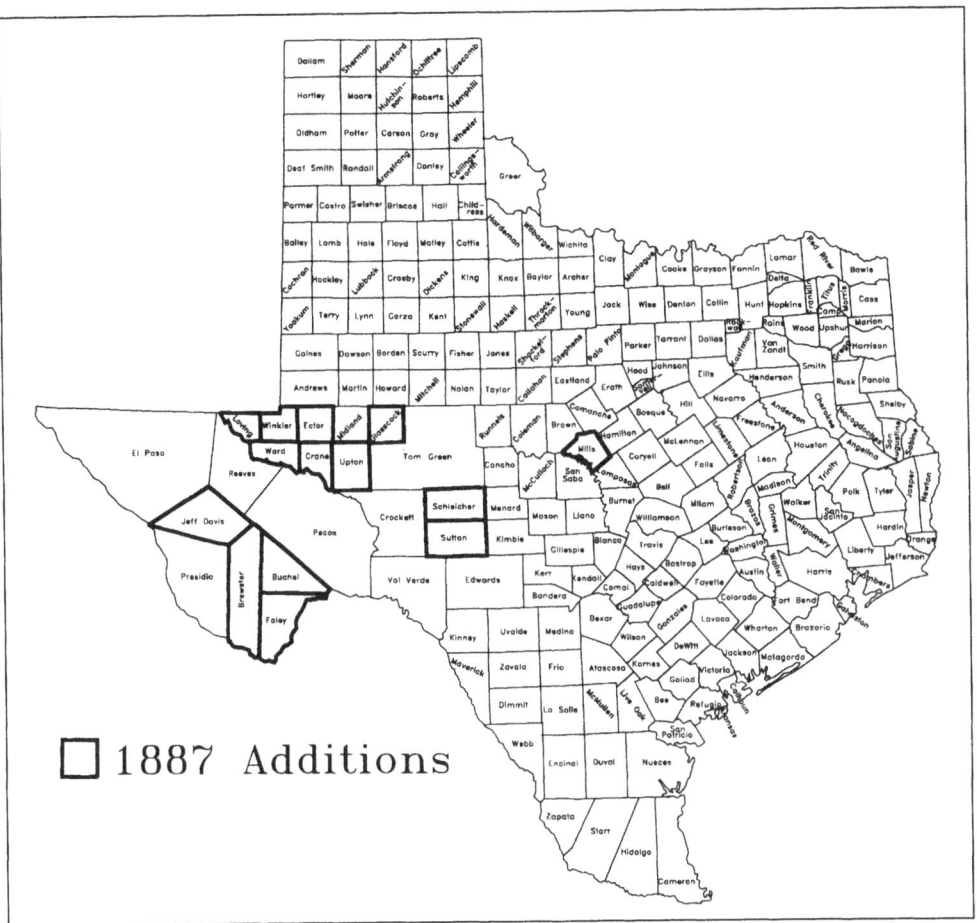

MAP 5-31. Changes in Texas counties, 1887. Map by Luke Gournay.

ished, their territory was placed in Brewster County, making it the largest county in Texas, with an area of 5,935 square miles.

Named: For Henry Percy Brewster, a South Carolinian who made his way to Texas as a young man in 1836. Under General Sam Houston, he fought in the Battle of San Jacinto. After becoming secretary of war of the Republic of Texas under Burnet, Brewster served in numerous other civic positions.

CRANE COUNTY

Created: From Tom Green County on February 26, 1887.

Organized: 1927, with the town of Crane named county seat.

Named: For William Carey Crane, an educator, who came from Virginia via Georgia and Mississippi. In 1836, he was president of Baylor University at Independence. As president of the Texas State Teachers Association, he advocated a reform of the Texas school system and establishment of the University of Texas.

ECTOR COUNTY

Created: February 26, 1887, out of Tom Green County.
Organized: January 6, 1891, when Odessa was made the county seat.
Named: For M. D. Ector, who came from Georgia in 1849 to practice law. During the Civil War, Ector rose to the rank of brigadier general in the Confederate army. Suffering a serious wound, he lost a leg, but later he served as a judge in various Texas courts.

GLASSCOCK COUNTY

Created: From part of Tom Green County, on April 4, 1887.
Organized: March 28, 1893, with Garden City as its county seat.
Named: For George W. Glasscock, a Kentuckian who came to the Municipality of Bevil (Jasper) in 1834. He alternated between serving in the military and surveying. Glasscock was instrumental in the formation of Williamson County, where Georgetown was named in his honor.

JEFF DAVIS COUNTY

Created: From a part of Presidio County on March 15, 1887.
Organized: May 24, 1887, with the town of Fort Davis as county seat. Fort Davis had been the seat of Presidio County, and the act creating Jeff Davis County specified Marfa as the new seat of Presidio County.
Named: For Jefferson Davis, president of the Confederacy for six years.

LOVING COUNTY

Created: From Tom Green County on February 26, 1887.
Organized: 1931, the last Texas county to be organized.
Named: For Oliver Loving, who came to Lamar County from Tennessee in 1845. With Charles Goodnight, he drove cattle to Colorado along a trail that came to bear their names. On one cattle drive, he was attacked and seriously wounded by Indians. Rescued by a group of Mexicans, he was taken for treatment to Fort Sumner in New Mexico. He died of gangrene at Fort Sumner, but his last plea to Goodnight was that he be buried on Texas soil. This wish was granted when Goodnight brought his body back to Weatherford for burial in 1868.

MILLS COUNTY

Created: March 15, 1887, from Brown, Lampasas, Comanche, and Hamilton counties.
Organized: September 12, 1887, with Goldthwaite chosen as county seat.

Named: For John T. Mills, who came from County Antrim, Ireland, to South Carolina, where he studied law. Around 1837, he came to Texas, serving in several judgeships.

SCHLEICHER COUNTY

Created: From Crockett County on April 1, 1887.
Organized: 1891, with Eldorado as the county seat.
Named: For Gustave Schleicher, born in Darmstadt, Germany, in 1823. He learned civil engineering in Germany and came to Texas in 1847, founding a commune called Bettina on the Llano River. After Indian attacks caused the venture to collapse, Schleicher moved to San Antonio, establishing a brilliant record. One of the most cultured men of Texas, he was recognized by United States President Garfield for his intellect, his precise speeches, and his innovative ideas. He is buried in the National Cemetery in San Antonio.

SUTTON COUNTY

Created: Out of part of Crockett County on April 1, 1887.
Organized: November 4, 1890, with Sonora as the county seat.
Named: For John S. Sutton, a native of Delaware who came to Texas in 1840. A military man, Sutton served his state and his country with great honor.

UPTON COUNTY

Created: February 26, 1887, as one of the twelve counties created from Tom Green County.
Organized: 1910, when the population numbered 501. The first county seat was Upland, but the railroad brought change. Coming through the county in 1911, the Panhandle and Santa Fe Railroad laid out the town of Rankin. Ten years later, Rankin replaced Upland as the county seat.
Named: For the brothers John and William Upton, who were born in Tennessee. By roundabout routes, both arrived in Texas around 1850. John died in the Civil War. William survived that war, becoming a businessman and Texas legislator.

WARD COUNTY

Created: From Tom Green County on February 26, 1887.
Organized: March 29, 1892, when Barstow was selected as county seat. A struggle over the location of the seat of government developed in the 1930s, when the Winkler oil field discovery caused Monahans to blossom. Monahans defeated Barstow to become the county seat in an election held on May 10, 1938. Barstow contested the result but lost its case in court the following year.

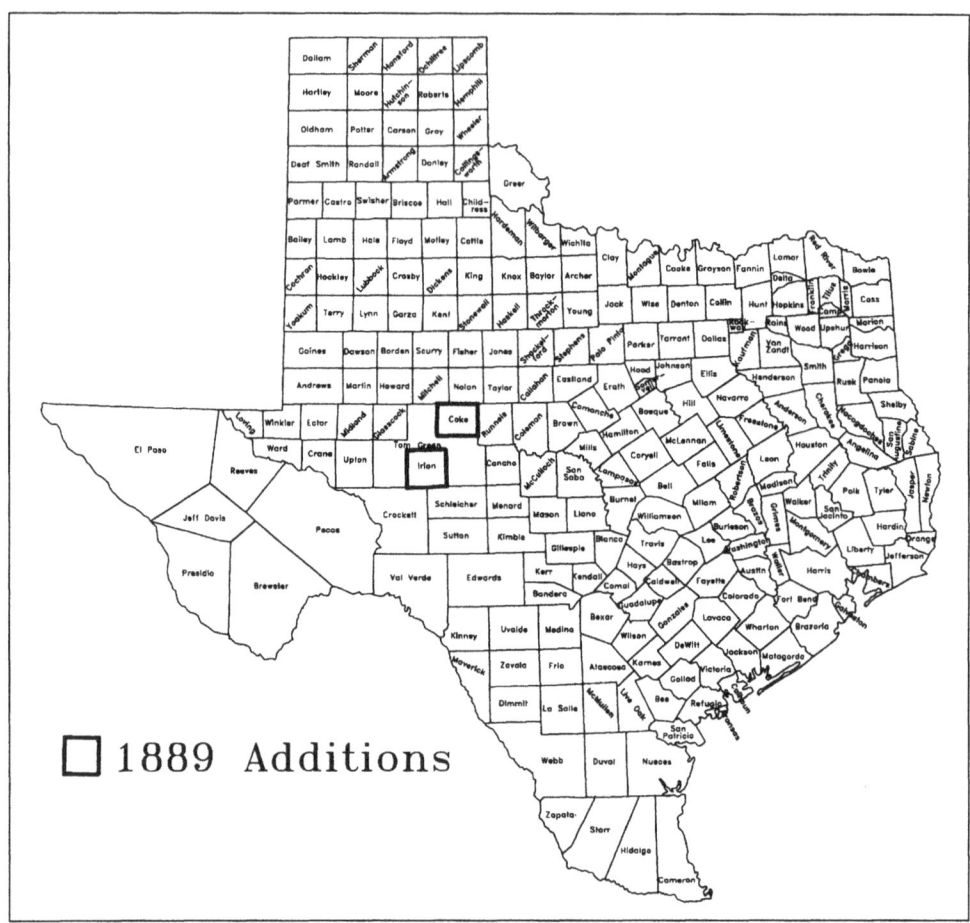

MAP 5-32. Changes in Texas counties, 1889. Map by Luke Gournay.

Named: For Thomas William Ward, an Irishman who came to New Orleans in 1835. A volunteer with the "New Orleans Grays," Ward lost a leg at the battle for Bexar in 1835. Unlucky with his limbs, he lost an arm in 1841 while firing a cannon in celebration of the Battle of San Jacinto.

WINKLER COUNTY

Created: February 26, 1887, out of Tom Green County, and attached to Reeves County for judicial purposes.
Organized: April 5, 1910. The first county court was held in the Kermit Hotel, as Kermit became the county seat. Two attempts by Wink to take the county seat, in 1927 and 1929, were unsuccessful.
Named: For Judge C. M. Winkler, a North Carolinian who came to Texas

in 1840. Wounded in the Civil War, he returned to activity in Texas affairs. His last duty was as a judge on the Texas Court of Appeals.

1889 Additions: Map 5-32

COKE COUNTY

Created: March 13, 1889, out of Tom Green County.
Organized: April 23, 1889, with Hayrick as the first county seat. In an 1891 election, the voters chose Robert Lee for that post, leaving Hayrick to dwindle to a ghost community.
Named: For Richard Coke, a Virginian who settled in Waco in 1850 to practice law. After fighting in the Civil War, he returned to be appointed district judge. Coke rose to be associate justice of the Texas Supreme Court before winning a gubernatorial election in 1873. Finally, he served two terms in the United States Senate.

IRION COUNTY

Created: Out of Tom Green County on March 7, 1889.
Organized: April 16, 1889, when Sherwood was selected as county seat. The Kansas City, Mexico and Orient Railroad was built in 1910, with stations at Mertzon, Suggs, and Monument. Having been bypassed, Sherwood dwindled, while Mertzon grew and became the county seat in the late 1930s.
Named: For Robert Anderson Irion, a Tennessee graduate of Transylvania University in Kentucky, who came to Texas in 1833. A member of the First Senate of the Republic, Irion became secretary of state in President Sam Houston's cabinet in 1837.

1891 Additions: Map 5-33

FOARD COUNTY

Created: March 3, 1891, out of parts of Cottle, King, and Knox counties and a large part of Hardeman County.
Organized: April 27, 1891. J. G. Witherspoon, a pioneer cattleman, petitioned the legislators for approval to organize the county. Playing politics well, he asked to name the county Foard after Maj. Robert Foard. Major Foard was the law partner of an influential member of the committee assembled to create the county. Witherspoon's ploy worked. Crowell, the largest town in the county, has been the county seat since organization.

STERLING COUNTY

Created: March 4, 1891, from Tom Green County. In the process of marking boundaries, a two-mile-wide gap was left between Irion and Sterling

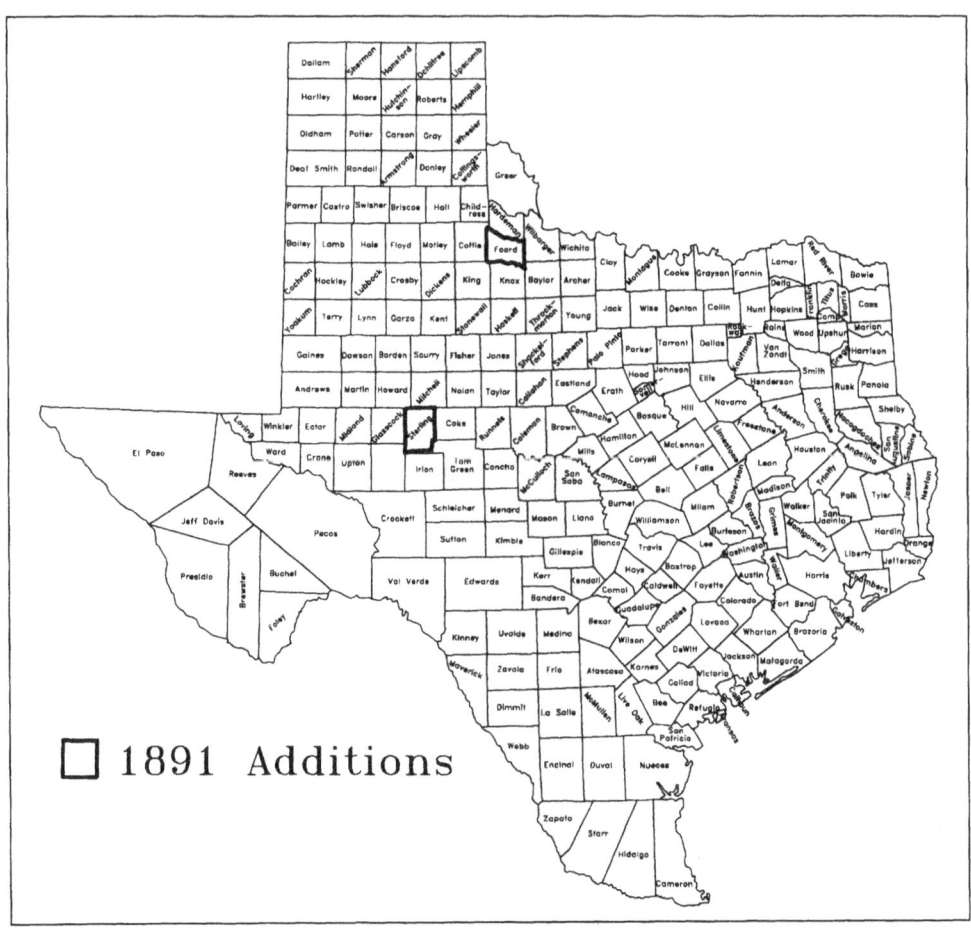

MAP 5-33. Changes in Texas counties, 1891. Map by Luke Gournay.

counties, making Tom Green essentially two counties, connected only by this channel.

Organized: June 3, 1891, with Sterling City (originally Montvale) named as county seat. Capt. W. S. Sterling, for whom the county is named, was a buffalo hunter and the first known settler in the area. Little else in known about Sterling, except that he left for Arizona when the buffalo herds diminished.

1896 to 1903 Activities: Map 5-34

GREER COUNTY

This county left Texas in 1896, remaining part of the United States.

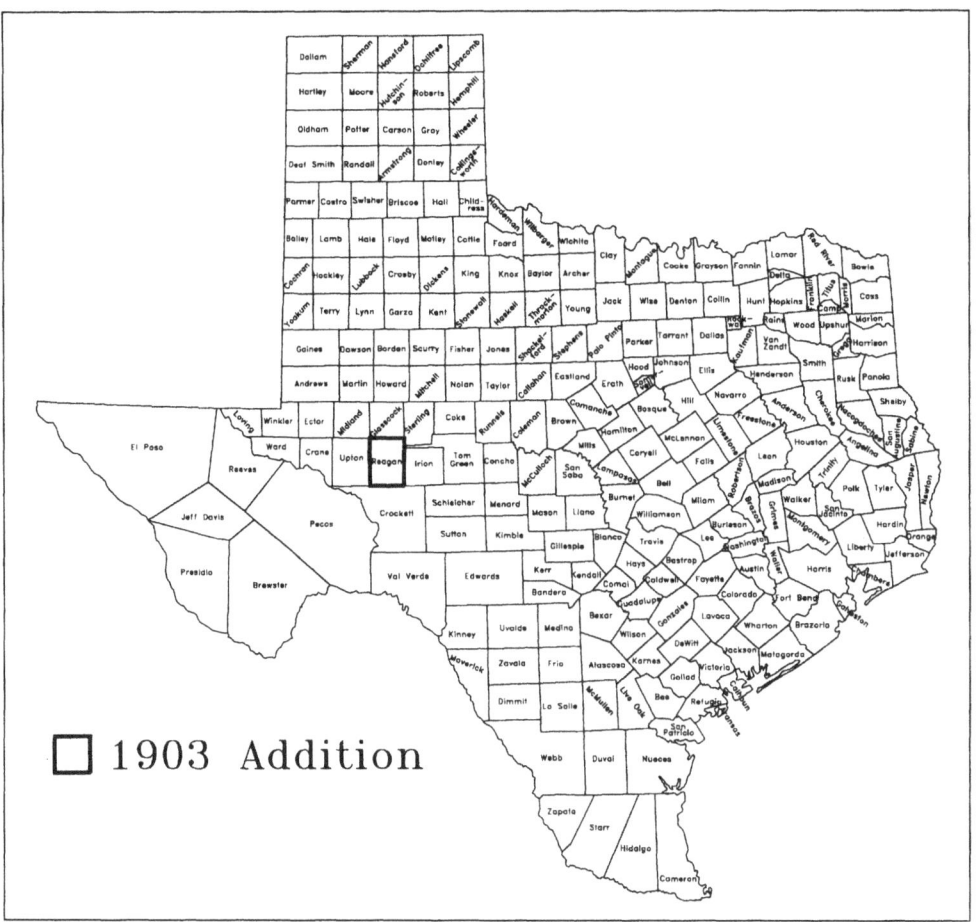

MAP 5-34. Changes in Texas counties, 1896 to 1903. Map by Luke Gournay.

BUCHEL AND FOLEY COUNTIES

These counties were abolished in 1897. Their territories were put into Brewster County.

ENCINAL COUNTY

Encinal County was abolished in 1899. It was absorbed by Webb County.

REAGAN COUNTY

Created: March 7, 1903, this county was the last to be formed out of the original Tom Green County. The new boundaries left a strange panhandle attached to the west side of Tom Green County. This anomaly, three miles wide and twenty-four miles long, remains today, with no direct route connecting this strip to the rest of the county.

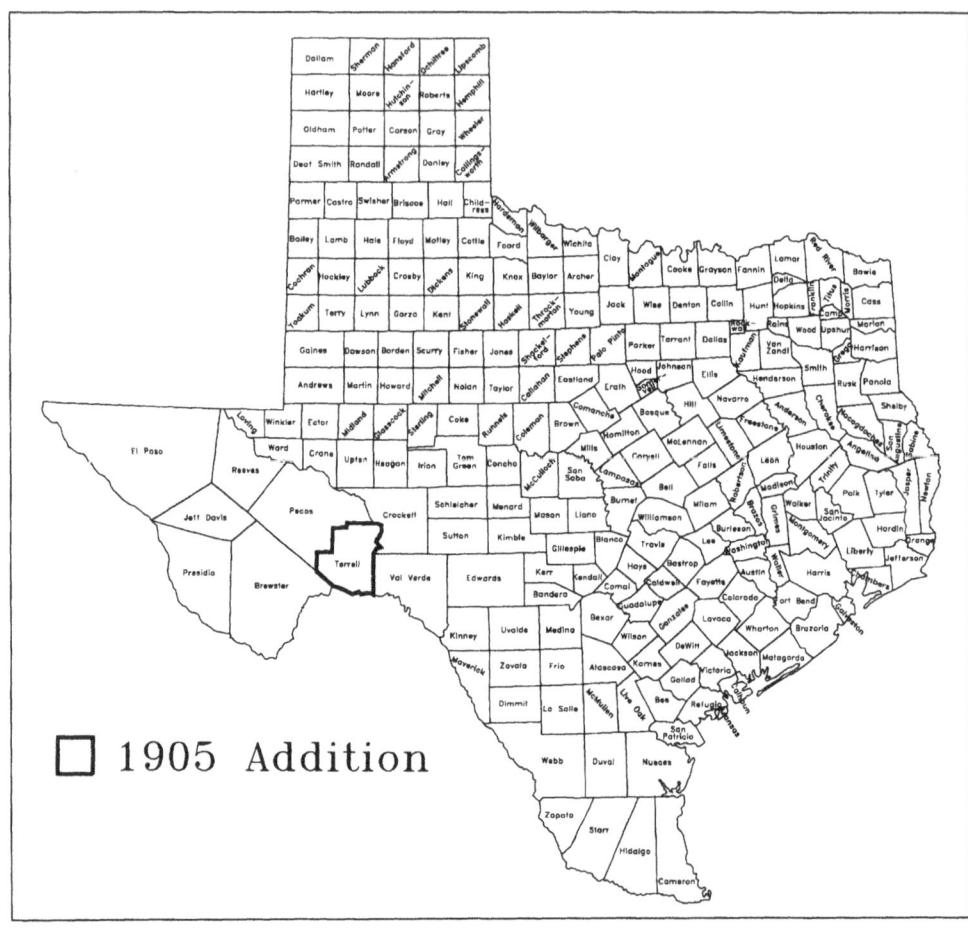

MAP 5-35. Changes in Texas counties, 1905. Map by Luke Gournay.

Organized: With Stiles as the county seat in 1903. Because a rancher would not sell right of way, the Orient Railroad was routed through Big Lake instead of Stiles in 1911. Big Lake became the county seat on May 23, 1925.

Named: For the illustrious John Henninger Reagan, who came from Tennessee in 1839. Reagan was a member of General Rusk's regiment that expelled the Cherokees from Texas, was the deputy surveyor for the Fannin Land District, was a captain in the militia of Nacodoches County, was a justice of the peace, a farmer, a cattle rancher, a Texas state legislator, and a Texas state judge. At Sam Houston's urging, he became United States congressman in 1857. Joining the Confederate government in 1861, Reagan served as postmaster general until the end of the Civil War. Captured by Federal troops, he was released in 1865, after which he appealed to United

States President Andrew Johnson for a more lenient policy toward the vanquished South. His final duty, at the request of Texas Governor James Stephen Hogg, was to chair the Railroad Commission of Texas.

1905 Addition: Map 5-35

TERRELL COUNTY

Created: April 8, 1905, from Pecos County.
Organized: With Sanderson as the county seat in 1905.
Named: For Alexander Watkins Terrell, a Virginian who moved to Texas in 1852. After fighting with the Confederate army, he fled to Mexico to serve with the French forces of Maximilian. Later elected to positions in the Texas House of Representatives, and the Texas Senate, he authored significant bills that improved juror selection criteria, created the Texas Railroad Commission, and revamped the system for nominating candidates for election. He also found time to be active in the Texas State Historical Association.

1911 Additions: Map 5-36

BROOKS COUNTY

Created: From Hidalgo, Starr, and Zapata counties on March 11, 1911.
Organized: 1912, when Falfurrias was chosen as county seat.
Named: For James Abijah Brooks. Brooks came from Kentucky in 1877, seeking employment as a cowboy in the San Antonio region. He worked as a Texas Ranger until 1906, when he settled in Falfurrias and engaged in farming. When Brooks County was created, Brooks was elected to the state legislature. *Falfurrias* is the Spanish word for a desert flower, the "Heart's Delight".

CULBERSON COUNTY

Created: As the fourth largest county in the state, it came out of El Paso County on March 10, 1911.
Organized: 1912, with Van Horn as county seat.
Named: For David B. Culberson, who came from Georgia to Jefferson, Texas, in 1856. After serving in the Confederate army, Culberson entered the political arena, serving in the Texas Senate and later in the United States Congress.

JIM WELLS COUNTY

Created: March 11, 1911, out of Nueces County.
Organized: 1912, with Alice as the county seat.
Named: After James B. Wells, Jr., who was born in Texas but earned a law degree at the University of Virginia. He worked in the Trans-Nueces area,

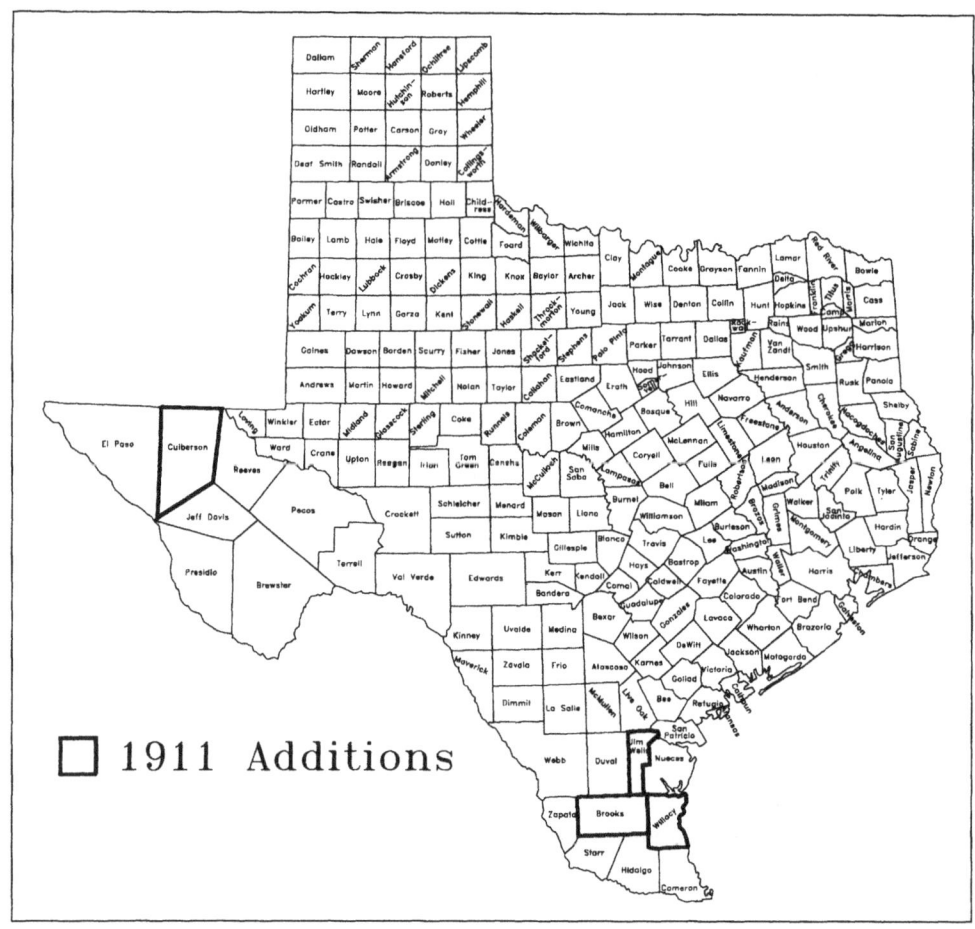

MAP 5-36. Changes in Texas counties, 1911. Map by Luke Gournay.

correcting fraudulent claims on Spanish and Mexican land grants. Wells played an important role in reducing friction between the Mexican and Anglo-American populations in South Texas.

WILLACY COUNTY

Created: March 11, 1911, from Cameron and Hidalgo counties.
Organized: 1912, when Sarita became the county seat.
Boundaries: Upon creation, the county extended from the Nueces boundary on the north to the Cameron boundary on the south. The birth of Kenedy County in 1921 caused a major upheaval in county boundaries and county seats. As a new and smaller Willacy County emerged, the county seat changed from Sarita to Raymondville, which formerly had been in

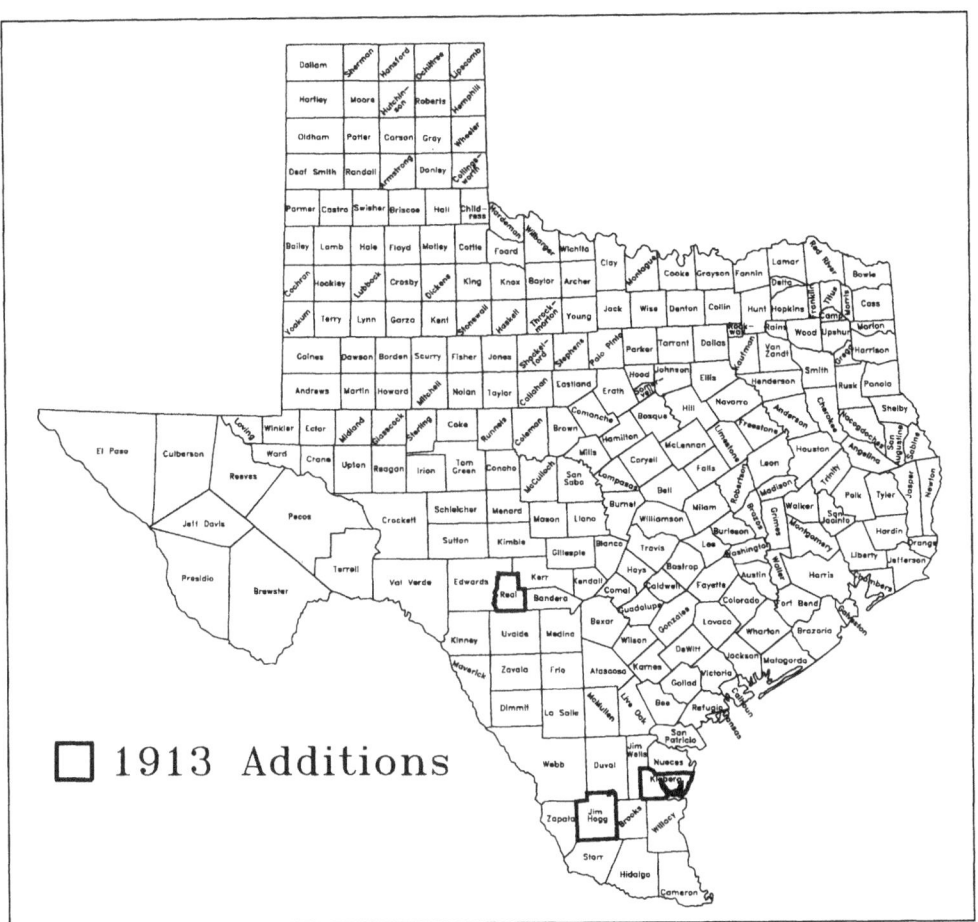

MAP 5-37. Changes in Texas counties, 1913. Map by Luke Gournay.

Cameron County. In a 1921 reorganization, Sarita became the seat of government in Kenedy County.

Named: For a Kentuckian, John G. Willacy, who came to Texas in 1892. He represented his district for many years in the Texas House of Representatives and Texas Senate.

1913 Additions: Map 5-37

JIM HOGG COUNTY

Created: March 31, 1913, from portions of Brook and Duvall counties.
Organized: 1913, when Hebronville, the principal town in the county, became the county seat.
Named: For James Stephen Hogg, who was the first Texas-born governor of

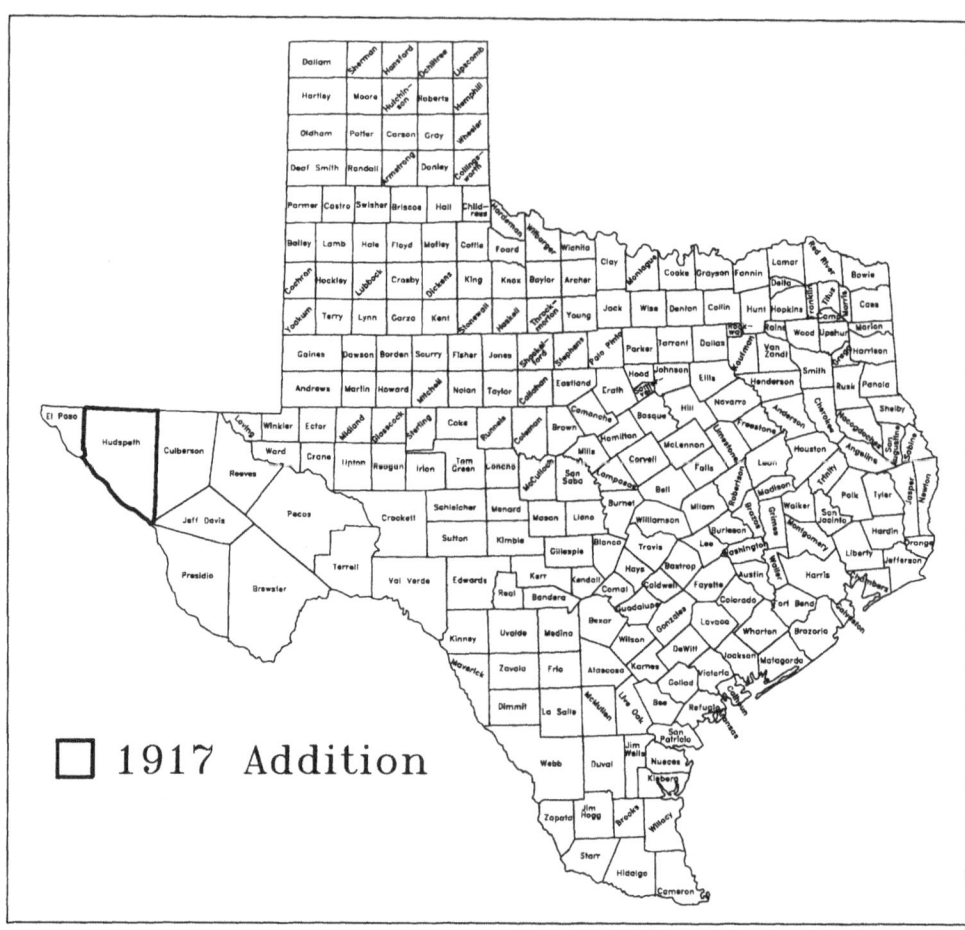

MAP 5-38. Changes in Texas counties, 1917. Map by Luke Gournay.

Texas. A leader in the movement for progressive democracy, Jim Hogg initiated numerous reforms considered beneficial to the state. Among these were: regulation of railroads by a commission, control over the issuance of corporate bonds, an Alien Land Law checking further land grants to foreign corporations, a new anti-trust law, and restrictions on the amounts of bonds that could be sold by counties and municipalities.

KLEBERG COUNTY

Created: February 27, 1913, out of Nueces County.
Organized: June 27, 1939, with Kingsville as the county seat.
Named: For Robert Justus Kleberg, an attorney who managed the King property. Kleberg married Alice Gertrudis King, the daughter of Richard King.

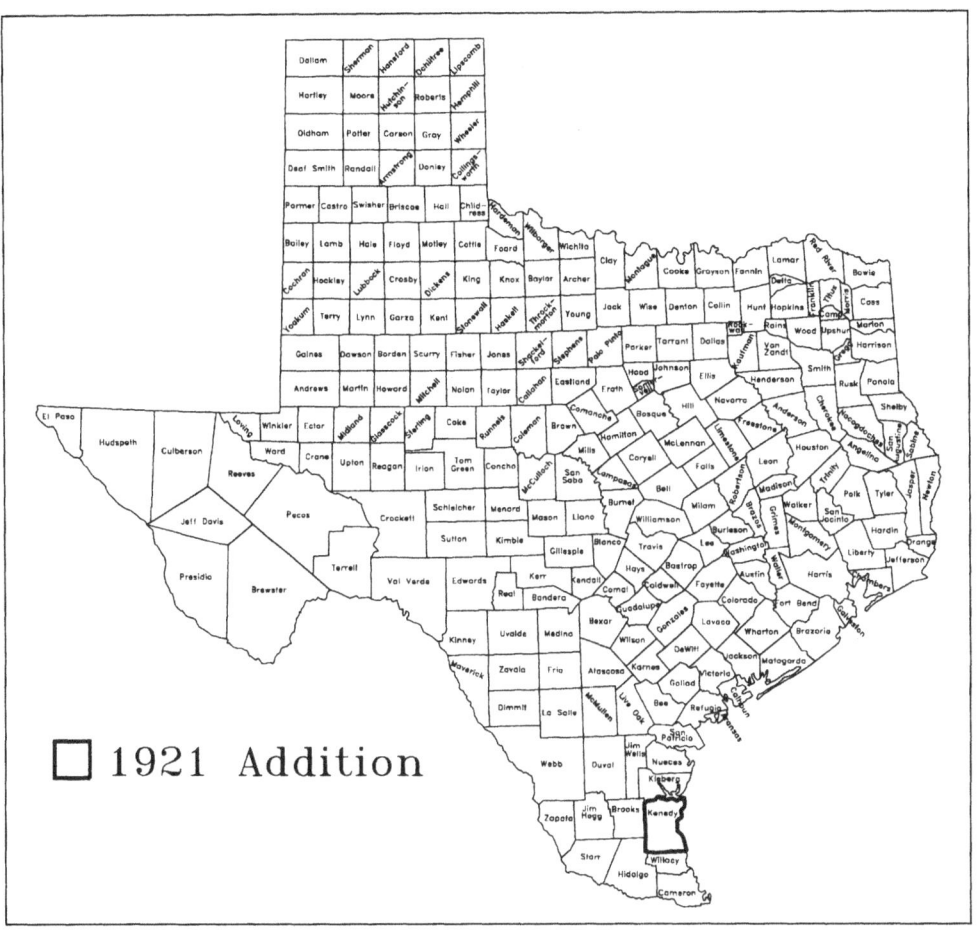

MAP 5-39. Changes in Texas counties, 1921. Map by Luke Gournay.

REAL COUNTY

Created: April 3, 1913, from parts of Bandera, Edwards, and Kerr counties.
Organized: 1913, with Leakey chosen for county seat. Leakey had been the seat of Edwards County before Real County's creation.
Named: For Justus Real, a native Texan who was born in Kerr County on May 7, 1860. After studies at Southwestern University in Georgetown, Texas, he returned to work on his father's ranch in 1884. By 1902, he was involved in civic and political life, serving as county commissioner, county judge, and county school superintendent, and as the lone Republican in the Texas Senate. Real died in 1944, in the house where he was born.

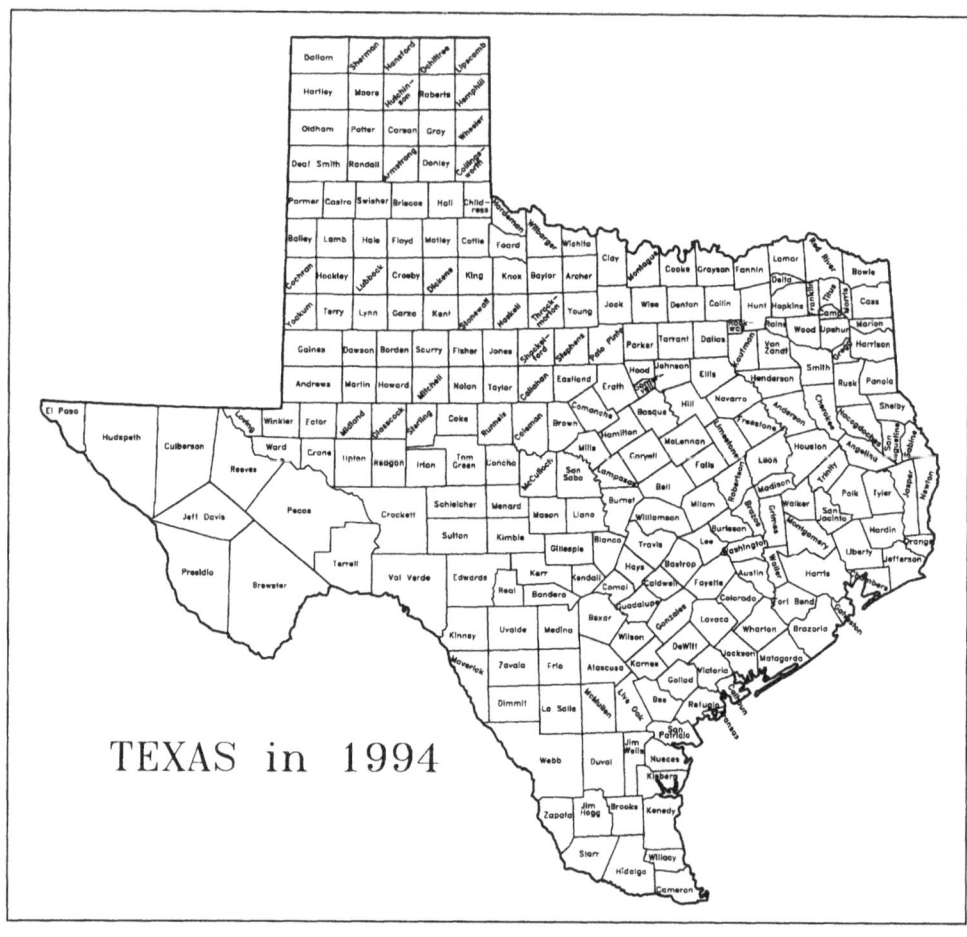

TEXAS in 1994

MAP 5-40. Texas in 1994. Map by Luke Gournay.

1917 Additions: Map 5-38

HUDSPETH COUNTY

Created: Out of the eastern section of El Paso County in February 1917. Hudspeth is the second largest county in Texas.

Organized: February 1917. Darlington, the first name suggested for the county seat, was changed to Turney, then to Hudspeth.

Named: For Claude Benton Hudspeth. A native Texan, born at Medina, Hudspeth had a long political career. Elected to the Texas House of Representatives, the Texas Senate, and the United States Congress, he was in office for twenty-nine consecutive years.

1921 Addition: Map 5-39

KENEDY COUNTY

Created: In 1921, out of parts of Willacy, Cameron, and Hidalgo counties, Kenedy is the most recently created county.
Organized: With Sarita as county seat in 1921. (See also Willacy County in 1911 Additions.)
Named: For Mifflin Kenedy, who was born in Pennsylvania in 1818. With a passion for boats, Kenedy became a sailor and a captain of steamers on domestic rivers and in the Gulf of Mexico. He also developed an interest in ranching, joining Richard King in establishing the King Ranch, which grew to 1,250,000 acres. Kenedy then turned to railroading and helped build a line from Corpus Christi to Laredo in 1876.

1994 Texas: Map 5-40

A fitting end to this book is the 1994 map of Texas, with its full complement of 254 counties. But the end of this book is probably not the end of county creation. Surely, in time, the sparsely settled Trans-Pecos region will attract people from outside its borders in increasing numbers. Many forces now building in the major cities could provide impetus for migration into these pristine lands.

When the time is ripe and the demand appears, there will be cause to draw yet another map of Texas.

Recommended Reading

Baker, D. W. C. *A Texas Scrapbook*. 1875. Reprinted Austin: Texas State Historical Association, 1991.

Baker, T. Lindsay. *Ghost Towns of Texas*. Norman: University of Oklahoma Press, 1986.

Barr, Alwyn. *Texas in Revolt*. Austin: University of Texas Press, 1990.

Edward, David B. *The History of Texas*. 1836. Reprinted Austin: Texas State Historical Association, 1990.

Fulmore, Z. T. *The History and Geography of Texas as Told in County Names*. Austin, Tex.: Steck, 1915.

Jackson, Jack; Robert S. Weddle; and Winston De Ville. *Mapping Texas and the Gulf Coast*. College Station: Texas A&M University Press, 1990.

Jordan, Terry G. *Texas: A Geography*. Boulder: Westview Press, 1984.

Kelsey, Mavis P., and Donald H. Dyal. *The Courthouses of Texas: A Guide*. College Station: Texas A&M University Press.

Muir, Andrew Forest, ed. *Texas in 1837*. College Station: Texas A&M University Press, 1958.

Reinhartz, Dennis, and Charles C. Colley. *The Mapping of the American Southwest*. College Station: Texas A&M University Press, 1987.

Spaw, Patsy McDonald. *The Texas Senate*. College Station: Texas A&M University Press, 1990.

Tarpley, Fred. *1001 Texas Place Names*. Austin: University of Texas Press, 1980.

Texas. General Land Office. Austin: Texas General Land Office, 1992.

Texas. General Land Office. *Guide to Spanish and Mexican Land Grants in South Texas*. Austin: Texas General Land Office, 1992.

Steen, Ralph W. *The Texas Story*. Austin: Steck, 1948.

Welch, June Rayfield. *The Texas Courthouses Revisited.* Dallas: GLAB Press, 1984.

In addition to this inviting list, one can discover a wealth of books devoted to the histories of individual counties. These publications by county historical societies are to be admired, for they preserve and display much of the best of Texas history.

Index

www.ingramcontent.com/pod-product-compliance
Lightning Source LLC
Jackson TN
JSHW020212031025
92012JS00020B/100